The Last Protégée

A Memoir of Uncertain Verisimilitude

Nancy Deeds Resler

Rebel ePublishers

Detroit   New York   London

Rebel ePublishers
Detroit, Michigan 48223

The Last Protégée
© 2015 by Nancy Deeds Resler

For information regarding permission, email the publisher at
rebele@rebelepublishers.com, subject line: Permission.

ISBN-13: 978-0692348963
ISBN-10: 0692348964

Book design by *Caryatid Design*
Cover design by *Littera Design*

Acknowledgements

I owe thanks to many who helped me along the way, but especially to Cynthia Ford, who first believed in my writing, and whose decades-long encouragement, intelligence and friendship has meant everything and inspired the work; to Kristine Pfliederer, DMH, whose wisdom and expertise urged me to grow and discover; to my husband, Ray, for his enduring patience and willingness to listen to my rage and despair during difficult periods in the writing; and to my teacher, Antonia Brico, for giving me her best and opportunities to excel well beyond my imagination -- and for teaching me the love of classical music.

Dream ~
Nancy: Tante, I'm not finished.
Antonia Brico: Thank you, Nancy

To my mother and father who were the beginning

Prelude

Misericord

Grandma is dying. She rocks back and forth, back and forth, holding a hand to the left side of her balding head. I don't see the baldness under the phthalo blue scarf knotted at the nape of her neck, to form a kind of cap. Her other hand adjusts the black patch now covering her left eye.

Grandma no longer hoes the weeds or gathers string beans and onions from her garden. She no longer chases down a squawking hen to ax off its head on the blood-stained stump out by the rude hollyhocks in preparation for the chicken and dumplings she loved to cook for Sunday dinner. No more tart sticks of rhubarb, salt-sprinkled; no more climbing sweet peas, that chaos of fragrance and color climbing her garden fence each spring.

I sit at her feet, my eyes hooded by fear. Is she contagious? I have eaten the chicken and dumplings prepared by her rough, brown hands; I have kissed the dry old mouth; I have slept beside her on the featherdown mattress. I love her, but I'm afraid.

"Sing to me, honeybunch," she croons. "Sing a song

for your old granny." She continues to rock. I sing
the song she loves to hear, "You are my sunshine, my
only sunshine." A smile spreads like a shadow over
her old weathered face.

An Exit, An Entry

BACA COUNTY BANNER
OBITUARIES

October 15, 1950

Minnie Amanda Deeds died in her home last night after a two-year battle with a brain tumor that had left her blind in one eye. Mrs. Deeds was the widow of Cyrus Edward Deeds, founding father of Pritchett and former owner of Jett & Deeds Hardware.

Minnie and Cyrus moved by covered wagon from Oklahoma to Baca County in 1915. There they lived with their three small children in a dugout, using the wagon cover as a roof, until Cyrus was able to develop his wheatfields and build the family home.

Minnie Deeds is survived by her three sons, Howard, Guy, and Buster, their wives, five grandchildren, and by the Baca County community where she had worked and lived for more than half a century.

*B*ands of winter light filter through the frosted glass panes and shine like sorrowful spotlights on the open casket. Walter Plague sings all four stanzas of *The Old Rugged Cross,* and I think my heart will break. For days after Grandmother's funeral, my dreams obstinately reflect the death mask of her pale, unanimated face.

It frightens and disturbs me, for it was not the face of the dearest friend of my childhood, but the face of a stranger.

BACA COUNTY BANNER
FAMOUS MUSICIAN TO HOLD AUDITIONS

November, 30th, 1950

Dr. Antonia Brico, internationally famous musician, teacher and conductor, will hold auditions next Saturday for students of voice and piano.

After graduating from the University of California at Berkeley in 1933, Dr. Brico studied with world-famous German conductor Dr. Karl Muck and in 1934, returned to New York to organize and conduct the New York Women's Philharmonic. In 1945, Dr. Brico moved to Denver where she organized the Denver Businessmen's Symphony, which she continues to conduct, and set up her studio on East 14th Avenue where she teaches conducting, piano, and voice.

Dr. Brico travels abroad each summer to meet and exchange ideas with other eminent teachers and musicians such as Bach scholar and humanitarian, Albert Schweitzer and noted Finish composer, Jean Sibelius.

"Not all of the talent lives in the cities," Dr. Brico said in a recent Denver Post interview. "This is why I travel the highways and byways to discover talented young people who would otherwise never have the opportunity to develop their musical gift."

Auditions will be held next Saturday in the home of Mrs. Martha Holt in Springfield. Those interested in scheduling an audition for themselves or their children should contact Mrs. Holt at JA5.4672.

A Roomful of Women

*P*ast the severely manicured hedges, up the front walk, past the sweet peas pinioned to painted trellises we march, I, an eleven-year-old child, and my entourage of women. Aunt Kay in her custom-made suit from Utah Woolen Mills, with its matching hat and striped fabric purse. Aunt Lucille, in her teal linen Easter outfit, set off by white patent pumps and bag. And Mother, slim and elegant, in her Lili Ann tweed suit with its pencil skirt and peplum jacket. All of the women wear gloves.

Martha Holt, the local banker's wife, has opened her home for auditions – a home considered elegant by Baca County standards. It has what is called "atmosphere," with its white wooden Venetian blinds, draped windows, closed doors. All of the furnishings are in tones of brown and burnt orange.

Brico herself answers the door. She wears a dark woolen skirt with smoke-green silk blouse, opaque hose, and lace-and-tongue black brogues. She stands, solid and superior. Her untamed mane of dirt-brown hair, fenced in by a thin silver band, accentuates the noble, strong features of her face. Roman nose, square, undeflected jaw, wide mouth and thick, masculine lips.

Wide-eyed and intimidated by this decidedly unfeminine and slightly ferocious personage, the group of women and I enter the close and sunless room.

Mother dissembles her nervousness and feelings of fierce protectiveness for her child by exhibiting a cool, natural poise. She sits on the sofa, tense, spine erect, her face composed to suggest a not unintelligent but accommodating nature, which is, in fact, not foreign to her.

Aunt Kay's eyes take in Brico's European style, her maleness, her uncoiffed hair, amused eyes, twinkling. Aunt Lucille breathes short, shallow breaths, luminous in her obvious desire to take my privileged place.

Directed to the cherry wood Baldwin spinet, I sit wrapped in protective mental fuzz made more dense by my extreme myopia – in spite of which, I intuitively recognize in the older woman, my Master.

"And now, little one," Brico sings, "what are you playing for me today?"

With a certain energy and enjoyment, I play "Nola" and something out of the Thompson Piano Series, Book IV or V, but surely with stiffness from nervousness and fright. The intensity of the Master, of what appears to be her unwavering concentration, exudes a palpable magnetism, at once attracting and repulsing. When I stop playing, Brico leans into the piano, fixing me with a hypnotic gaze.

... silence, stillness, broken only by the metronomic ticking of the grandfather clock in the hall ...

"The child is gifted," Brico says at last to Mother, "possibly enormously so. But there is a very great deal of work to do if she is to realize that gift." She continues, "Her hand position, all wrong. Technique, all wrong. I can help her, but we need to start all over and the child will need to work very hard." Brico returns her mesmeric gaze to me, patting my hand.

Mother heeds details to consider, the long-term commitments involved: one, probably two, one-hour lessons twice a month when Brico comes to town. The cost, a staggering $10 an hour. A fortune compared to the 75 cents an hour Miss Finney charges.

Driving home, tension resolves into relief and merriment. Aunt Kay critiques Brico's manner and dress, finding humor in every gesture and thread. Aunt Lucille giggles, but I know that secretly she feels the awe of one who has experienced a rare Presence. Mother enters into the gaiety, keeping her fears for me locked deep inside; free-floating anxieties for her child's future under the influence of this strange and powerful woman.

My spirits soar in the company of these women, and too, at what pleasure the recounting of the event will provide my father who waits at home. And so I retreat into my own world and dream, clinging to the idea of being gifted, possibly enormously so.

The Surrogate Mothers

A Problem of Loving

Dr. Brico says she was so determined to be a good Mamma that she put Nancy Lou to bed three times a day. I think Philip Wylie should hear about this.

Excerpt, *Baca County Banner*, November 1950

Today I took a lesson from Dr. Brico in Springfield. She bawled me out and told me the story of her life.

~ Diary, March 12, 1951

I took another lesson today from Dr. Brico. She thinks I'm a real musician and she wants me to go to Denver for two weeks and get a free lesson every day and watch her conduct. Tonight I parted my hair in the middle.

~ Diary, March 26, 1951

Today I took another lesson from Dr. Brico. She said I had really improved. I go to Denver in two weeks and two days.

~ Diary, April 9, 1951

I had my first train ride today to Denver. Tonight I went with Dr. Brico and Mrs. Page (the woman who lives with her) to my first opera. It was *La Traviata*. It was really good.

~ Diary, April 25, 1951

Today I had two lessons, a piano lesson with Dr. Brico

and a solfege lesson with Mrs. Page.

~ Diary, April 27, 1951

Today I left at 4:00 a.m. for Lamar to catch a bus. We got to Denver at 11:30 a.m. I am staying with Mr. and Mrs. Webster. Dr. Brico says that Mrs. Webster has a heart of gold. I don't know why I can't go on staying with Dr. Brico and Mrs. Page.

~ Diary, July 1, 1951

Today Dr. Brico, Judy Collins, Gladys Kimball, Dr. Brico's friend, and I went to Eliches. After a few rides, we saw the theater play "The Legend of Sarah." The Browns from Springfield will come up tomorrow and I will ride home with them on Sunday. I can't wait to get home.

~ Diary, July 4, 1951

We got to Springfield today at 3:30 p.m. Mother, Daddy, Eddy and Teresa were waiting for me. I was sure glad to be home again.

~ Diary, July 8, 1951

GERTIE WEBSTER

Were I to render the image of her that comes fullest to mind, I would work with loud, raw color – vivid, but with a limited palette – pigment squeezed wet from the tube. The coarseness of composition augmented by a background of angular shapes, suggesting common, unrefined elements. And areas of harsh chiaroscuro, as in twilit basements and dark stairwells.

It is summer, and standing out amongst all of this is Gertie. She wears blue jeans belted with a too-long belt, buckled and threaded back through the belt

14

loops, the legs rolled up in wide cuffs above white bobby sox and white lace shoes. Her short-sleeved shirt, pocketed, bleached and blued white, starched so that the tops of the cuffs stand up in little points on the ridge of her biceps.

I might paint her in full figure profile, standing as I mostly remember her, watering the lawn at 1515 Grant, conscientious in her role as property caretaker, building manager.

A painting, however, cannot give full expression to the image in memory, and a bucolic scene of stillness cannot correspond even remotely to the idea of Gertie.

Her hand holds a watering hose and a full flow of water arcs, falls onto the grass. Directly above the mouth of the hose, and echoing its gushing stream, is Gertie's mouth. She is "yakking it up" with some "old bat" who lolls (unseen in my painting) on the iron bench at the edge of the lawn. Or "shooting the breeze" with Al, the postman, or with a complete stranger who happens by. Or with Frank, the skinny, bespectacled nephew of old Mrs. Booth, one of several unappealing beaux Gertie seeks out to shepherd my way.

WEB

To anchor the scene onto the canvas, it is necessary to create a companion piece depicting Web. He sits, below ground level in a dark room, lit as though for the blind. His weight gives one end of the brown frieze sofa a permanent sag.

15

The scene is painted in raw umbers and burnt sienna, but perhaps most appropriately drawn in charcoal, so as to fully capture the artist's feelings of darkness and revulsion that are now also tinged with pathos. Web wears gray twill pants and a slightly lighter gray cotton shirt, long-sleeved and unornamented except for two patch pockets in front.

Web, strangely, remembers himself as some kind of dandy, alive with success as a photographer, shooting portraits of children at Christmas and Easter. How he tossed the ball, the furry rabbit into the air; how the child laughed, how he squeezed the black bulb of the camera at just the right moment; the parent's pleasure. Simple, tired stories, and yet how, in my mind, they augment the idea of some perverse history. I feel there is something disturbingly womanly about him.

Now, he sits in the basement gloaming. He sits, silent and quiescent, a heap of pale impossibilities. Because it is still summer, the basement windows stand ajar and he sits, passively listening to the constant chatter from above.

At the time of this memory, stormed by adolescent emotions, I desire to be neither above, where Gertie's incessant and senseless chatter would besiege and render me glaringly visible, nor in the nether regions, where Web would attempt to regale me with stories of his dead past.

Longing to be neither here nor there but to be completely elsewhere, each night and late into the mornings, I manage this through a deep and dreamless sleep, believed by some, to be the most perfect state of existence.

BRICO

My portrait of Brico, a large oil on canvas, would impress you with its musical patterns and its obvious source of light. The overall impression is a portrait done by Frank Auerbach: the rich palette, the rhythmic texturing, the off-plumb likeness of her! Modern edginess is apparent and yet, it is a sense of timelessness that informs the whole picture.

I capture her in profile: the magnificent Italian nose, the determined Dutch jaw, the gaze penetrating even as it focuses on a subject outside the frame of the work. Of course, no portrait of her is complete without attention to the sweep of dark hair with its silver streak running back from a defined widow's peak.

She has a strong aversion to hair, her own or another's, that falls onto the face. She will stop a conversation or a lesson to tuck errant strands behind the ears of a student whose features may be shadowed by a threatening forward style.

As for herself, Brico wears a slim sterling silver band in an attempt to restrain her own hair, keeping it well away from her face. And giving her a look of intensity, boldness and a sense of undeflected purpose.

Had I chosen to paint a scene rather than a portrait of Brico, she would be in her studio, seated at one of her nine-foot Steinway Grands. On the fireplace mantel, busts of composers, notably those of Beethoven and Sibelius. Photographs of other composers and many pieces of original art, begged and coaxed from friends on her visits around the world, cover the studio walls.

If I painted this scene in the morning, long before dawn, Brico would be seated at one of the Steinways, a manuscript of Rachmaninoff's Piano Concerto in D minor propped up on the music stand, opened to the third movement, the most troublesome one for her massive, but still beautiful, hands. A side table near the tufted piano bench on which she sits would bear small dishes of fruit: prunes, figs or dates, pieces of apple or pear.

Had I chosen to paint a scene later in the day, you would see her at the same piano, but this time with a child on the tufted bench, earnest, full of the desire to please. Perhaps the child has practiced, and the lesson is going well, with Brico expansive, encouraging, gentle in her corrections of hand position, phrasing.

A painting of a child surviving a lesson that is not going well (and there were certainly these) would without doubt be more dramatic. The child tries but fails, tries again – still it does not go well.

Brico no longer smiles, or drips encouragement like a rich baklava. She brandishes her baton and, once or twice, raps the little hands as they flounder on the keys. The air is electric with tension and the child's fear.

If the child bursts into tears, which is more than likely, Brico throws down the baton and folds the child into her arms. She consoles her, *dolcemente*, urging her on, stressing the importance of discipline and practice, of the brilliance of the future and of the fame they seek together.

"I am," she croons to the anxious child," your musical mother. Together, Little One, we will rise to the heights of Parnassus."

*N*anny Lou, Nanny Lou, rouse Schmidt!" calls Gertie. "Get up, my sweetie," she echoes, translating. She sails through the door, calling me to a wakefulness I long to reject. In an effort to light on a diminutive familiar for my name, she has, unfortunately, decided on "Nanny Lou." It repulses me and makes me feel like a goat.

"We dasn't let her sleep all day!" I have become accustomed to Gertie's Pennsylvania Dutch verb contractions, but not her voice, which now plays in the air.

It is the annoying quality of a tinny accordion, like the hateful sound of Myron Foren's accordion on the Lawrence Welk TV show she and Web insist on watching. The show grates, with Myron's corny songs on the accordion, or Big Tiny Little playing his ragtime tunes on the piano. Or Lawrence Welk himself with his tiresome catch-phrases, "Ana-1, ana-2," as he indicates the beat for his big band orchestra and later, "Wunnerful, wunnerful."

Gertie raves about Myron, whose physique and the

way he hops around with that awful accordion slung around his body, makes me think of a mosquito. She encourages me to learn to play her small instrument that she pulls out of the closet and straps to my body, but I will not.

It is only a matter of minutes before I hear the door open and close again. Web takes up the call, "Rouse Schmidt, Nanny Lou," he cries, walking past the door of my room once or twice before again settling himself comfortably on the sofa.

When I finally *rouse* myself and stumble out into the kitchen, I find a white bakery bag full of bear claws, the pastry Gertie knows I love. Its yeasty, sweet body will appease me and also Gertie is not much of a cook. Bear claws do their part to fatten the hungry lamb.

On one of these days, in the late afternoon, the sun falls across the room giving it an eerie underwater feel. Web is on the sagging end of the sofa. I dump my pastry-laden body into the big chair on the far side of the room, hating myself, my body. Hating that I don't have the energy to escape before Web begins one of his stories.

Startled out of my ennui by a choking sound, Gertie has come into the house, probably to pull our frozen dinners from the "frig." Web sits, gagging and choking, his eyes bulging from his distorted face. Gertie runs in and sits beside his convulsing body. She reaches in and takes his tongue in a kind of stranglehold. The sight paralyzes me. Web sits gagging and struggling.

"Heart," Gertie says to me. "He dasn't swallow his tongue. It won't last long."

She sits calmly, grasping his tongue and talking to Web in a quiet voice. Later she tells me that these attacks are not uncommon.

It seems strange then, as it does now, that no doctor is called in or even consulted.

*B*ecause it is summer and because student recitals occur in July, my stay here will drag on much longer than in the winter months when visits generally last only two or three days. Every day will be apportioned according to lesson time and a schedule of practice.

On lucky days, when Brico has an appointment downtown, I am left alone in the studio to practice on my favorite concert grand – willing to be seduced by its curvaceous form and its deeply resonant tone – by its aura of virility. On the luckiest of these days, rare days filled with an old promise, I sit mesmerized at the keyboard for eight to ten hours.

The practice will tell in the next day's lesson and my solo recital at the end of the week, but the deeper reward is the righteous one I feel from my sore (but not bleeding) fingers. I have read about a Russian pianist who practiced for many days until his finger bled.

It reminds me of Dostoevsky, of what I see as the superior Russian soul. It is a symbol of some kind of spiritual zeal, a symbol of purity. It is a matter of small sadness to me that however long I practice, my fingers never bleed.

Many days are less lucky, which means I am left in the company of Gertie or Web with hours to secretly nurse my adolescent depression. Gertie attempts to lure me into her world of teenage flirtations with Al the postman, or the Hull photo delivery fellow, one of her associates from work, or especially with Doug, a Continental Trailways bus driver. This last taking on something of a romantic obsession with her. Doug is in his early forties, tall and dark, his good looks enhanced by his pleated and pressed gabardine uniform.

Looking back it is easy to see how appealing Doug is in contrast to the blancmange of Web.

Doug is one of the regular drivers for my route. Since meeting him, Gertie talks incessantly about him when we are alone. "Oooh la la, Doug," she says, rolling her eyes around and grinning foolishly.

She has memorized Doug's schedule and from then on, my every trip is coordinated with Doug's run whenever possible. We always leave the apartment early to ensure that she has time to stand and "chew the fat" with him as he stands at the bus door punching tickets of boarding passengers. I can see her there, standing, "shooting the breeze," laughing, as she throws back her head, revealing a large goiter.

When Gertie discovers that Doug has a son, she nags until he gives her a 4"x6" photo of sixteen-year-old Bennett. "Oooh la la," she twitters, rolling her eyes in that repulsive way as she hands me the photo – a photo I can only associate with feelings of humiliation.

Once on board, I pull out my coin purse where I have secreted Roger's class ring with its dingy wrapping of masking tape, sized to fit the third finger of my left hand. Because the ring must be kept secret from Brico and my father, it is comforting to keep it also from Gertie.

The ring is large and bulky and gold, ornately carved with deep gashes to elevate the crest. I especially like the impressive Akron High School insignia, with its glint of royal purple. Roger has a questionable reputation. He smokes and "carouses" and has a scar on his right cheek. Also, he is two years older, and so must remain concealed from my father, who desires to protect me, and will not allow me to go on a date until I turn sixteen, but, too, by Brico who, on the subject of boys, stresses the necessity of "waiting" until I am "famous," when I will be able to choose from the crème de la crème.

Meanwhile, I keep the ring. It signifies a place of belonging on the otherwise liminal threshold of my flowering adolescence.

I leave them there to form a kind of frieze: Brico with her students and orchestra; Al with his bulging mailbag of letters; Doug with his son and his red Continental Trailways bus. I leave Web with his heart attacks and memories as he sits in darkness at that time of day when the light falls obliquely through the small high windows, making him appear slightly phosphorescent, like some exotic middle ocean predator.

23

And, as much as leaving Web, I leave Gertie watering the lawn out front, "yakking it up" with a tenant, or her head thrown back in full chortle. Leave her there with her heart of gold.

What the Child Wanted

I want not to be a puppet. I want not want to be expected to perform in exchange for love. I want to be believed in absolutely and only as I am.

To hear the mother's wisdom, her self-confidence, I want to experience the mother's extreme gentleness and terrible power. Most of all, I want to be held in an unhurried, unembarrassed embrace and know that I am the mother's eternal and only treasure.

What is this blue pain throbbing in the vicinity of my heart?

A Repertoire of Eros

B in Black Velvet

I catch her profile; the strong Italian jaw, pensive with anticipation and nerves, the noble head held high above the prim white collar. The profile of a Roman general, I think. The black gown, flared to full-length, conceals the black lace-up brogues I know she wears over her opaque woolen hose. From here, I can barely make out the wedge of ivory hair at her brow, glowing like a casket of pearls, as it flows back under her silver headband.

The applause gradually fades into a few coughs and a scatter of murmurs. House lights dim. Now I can see her body tense, see her poised baton forming an extension of her crisp white cuff. Every eye is on her. One breathless moment, then, suddenly, her body lunges into the music, is released, and she carries me with her into another world.

Tonight it is *Finlandia.*

O, the magic and wonder of her, the power and the glory of her!

The noble features, now soft, heavy with a different desire, her flush-brown hair unmanned, alive above the plunging *décolleté* of blue velvet, her maternal bosom now voluptuous. The full, coarse lips, dripping venous red, the controlling gaze of the teacher now the stare of a stranger. Her body of curves and round shapes spreads itself over the stallion black of the Steinway and the music begins.

> ***"Curves are so emotional"***
> - Piet Mondrian

God or demon, Zeus or Medusa? My body streams with foreign emotions: with fear, with a symphony of rioting, creative desire. I plant a single conciliatory kiss on one rude-blushed cheek.

Steinways and Stallions

Today I got to Denver about 2:30. Mother and Daddy drove me up. I was a special guest on The Ray Perkins Show. Tonight Mother and Daddy got to hear my rehearsal with the orchestra – real good.

~ Diary, March 3, 1954

Today at 11:30 a.m., Dale Morgan recorded an interview with Dr. Brico, Mother, Daddy, and me. It will be on the air tomorrow eve at 7:45 p.m. Was on the June Sterling show as a guest. Mother and Daddy went home.

~ Diary, March 4, 1954

Today they interviewed me at The Denver Post and took my picture. Went to Phipps Auditorium and tried the piano. I like it fine.

~ March 8, 1954

Today Louis and I went to Well's warehouse to try pianos. Was on the Jody Noles TV show. Went off fine. Sure like TV.

~ March 9, 1954

This afternoon I practiced at Phipps. We're going to use their piano at the auditorium. Went to dress rehearsal tonight. Did good. The orchestra stood and clapped for a long time. Dr. Brico hugged me.

~ March 10, 1954

Today Dr. Brico and her good friend, Mrs. Davis, took me to eat at Tiffin Inn. $2.35 for half a chicken. Then I rested. Debut tonight. Very successful. Mrs. Davis gave a party at Bauer's for me. Very good crowd at concert.

~ March 11, 1954

*T*he Steinway Grand and Louie Stojowsky, in close proximity. The piano silent, in a sacred waiting; the man, silent above roiling inner oceans. The instrument looming large, more, in the enormity of its potential. And I, the child, eleven – or fourteen – caught somewhere in between, but feeling only the magnetic pull of the piano, its beauty, its unlimited possibility.

*L*ittle one," Brico cries, tapping her long blonde baton on the curve of the keyboard's shoulder, "the Mozart!"

I shuffle the books of music on the stand in front of me and pull out the Mozart A-Major concerto, comforted by the familiar feel of its smooth, pale cover, the reassurance of its well-worn pages – and the double gold stars on its upper right-hand corner.

Out of the corner of my eye, I see Louie slumped in a chair and feel his silence spreading over the room like a shadow. His presence disturbs me. He seems too close, even when he sits at the far end of the room. He looks so intense, I feel that the occasional strike of Brico's baton sends a shudder through his body. I think then that Louie is a priest and I can't

32

understand why he's spending time around the studio.

Many years later, I find a web article published in the Polish Music Journal written by Joseph A. Herter on Sigismond Stojowski, Louie's father and Brico's piano teacher in New York in the late 1920s. The article explains some of the mystery of Louie: he lived in Denver between 1952 and 1955 and taught Latin in the Denver Public Schools. During that time, the article states, he also studied piano and conducting with Brico. Not a priest, although he had planned to become a priest in his early years.

The lesson is going well. My playing infused with a passion that (thinking back on it now) seems to give off a kind of incandescence. I try not to see Louie leaning into the music as I play, as though he wants to feel the emotion I am pouring into it – that he wants to be a part of that beauty with its dazzling surface and dark underbelly.

He wants to be the Steinway, I think. He wants to possess its black glossy beauty, its handsome ivory keyboard, its enormous possibility. I can feel, even at a distance, his body, tight with the tension between the light created through the music and his darkness submerged. I break off playing, feeling confused and disturbed.

Brico's baton strikes the arm of the Steinway. I take up again from the measure where I had left off.

"Tomorrow," Brico tells me once the lesson is over, "Louie will go with you to Well's Steinway warehouse. They have hundreds of pianos there. Just think, hundreds of Steinway pianos! Can you imagine?

You must play on all of them until you find the one with an action that you like best. Take all of the time that you need, Little One. You must not hurry. Remember, choosing the right piano will be critical to a fine performance on Thursday night."

Why can't I just use the piano at Phipps Auditorium, I wonder. I like it just fine. And why must she call me "Little One"? I'm fourteen years old! Why does she always make of me the child? And where is this warehouse anyway? We'll have to go by bus and I don't at all like the idea of going with Louie. Why can't Dr. Brico take me? She seems always to be palming me off onto someone else. Besides, Louie is strange. Black hairs sprout from his body everywhere. I don't like being alone with him. And how can I choose a piano among "hundreds"? Having to choose among a dozen would be hard enough, I think.

*T*he city bus proceeds.
Louie frightens me, although I cannot say why. Exactly. Maybe it is because he has a "used" smell. Maybe it is his thick eyebrows that shade his face like a visor; or the hairs that grow right out of his nostrils and ears; or the strings of black hair on his head, too long, looking slightly soiled, unmanaged. Her mother would not put up with that, I think, and it makes me wonder just what kind of mother Louie had anyway.

Louie is not much taller than I, but he seems very strong without being muscular. His left shoulder looks larger and higher than his right, which makes him walk in a slanting kind of way. As though he just might fall over with the next step. I worry that if he falls he will fall against me, or that he will fall completely and I will have to pick him up. I recoil at the thought of having to touch him.

The warehouse, when we enter, reminds me of my father's barn, his prize white-faced Herefords – but mostly of his herd of stallions. So many pianos! A herd of black Steinways! I squint, peering through the air that is dry and thick with dust motes. The pianos stand, all merged together, a silent mass, still and mostly shrouded in shadow. A pool of thickening mucus gathers at the back of my throat, and it seems to me that my nostrils are swelling and closing. I feel congested with a foreign emotion and cannot breathe. I think suddenly of the John Payne western movie when I heard the cowboy in the black hat shout, "Stampede!"

Louie waits, watching from within the shadow of the doorway. I am aware of him standing there, sensing how he wants to "comfort" me. I do not want comfort from Louie! For another moment, I stand frozen, then turn and run back, past Louie standing in the doorway, out into the brave sunlight of the crisp March day.

"Let's go," I say. "I prefer the piano at the auditorium."

Louie merely nods.

Brico has just finished with Suzanne's voice lesson when Louie and I walk in.

"And so, Little One," she says. "Did you find a piano? Did you play on all of them?"

"I prefer the one already at Phipps Auditorium," I say, glancing anxiously in Louie's direction. He nods and smiles. He believes it is a seraphic smile, but to me, it looks like the smile of a conspirator.

I look quickly away.

Hour of the Star

The years of lessons, the hours of practice – the mantle of B's great desire, which I wear, believing it my own – Dad hugging me and saying again, "Hitch your chariot to a star, Sissy." Given the unwavering support of family, the determination and special attentions of B, my reasonable talent and willing industry in practice; given the expectations of us all, some small success could hardly be avoided.

And so, soon the Mozart; and then, months later, the audition with the symphony board, and my name added to the select few soloists to perform with the Denver Businessmen's Symphony in their sixth season. The young orchestra, I, the young performer, the virile and dedicated teacher and conductor: the potent trio.

Gertie procures a retired photographer who comes to the apartment and shoots six takes of me, the young protégée, sitting at my Acrosonic, imported for practice from my Akron home. In the photos, the piano looks like a toy. I wear my eighth-grade graduation dress, a white v-necked frock with short puffed sleeves and a gathered skirt. Around my neck is a hideous rhinestone choker. The proofs capture a young woman with an English, almost aristocratic profile, shoulder-length, unimportant hair, but, indeed, very fine hand position, the knuckles raised like the roof of a barn. She sits, staring dreamily into her future.

Local musical talent is not ordinarily in short supply, even in the mid-west, even in Baca County; but protégés are rare enough, even in Denver, so the editors of several counties send photographers and reporters to capture the story, printed on the front pages of *The Baca County Banner* and *The Sterling News Reporter*, and in *The Denver Post*, as an item in their "Arts & Entertainment" section.

FORMER PRITCHETT GIRL IS CITED AS OUTSTANDING PIANIST WITH FUTURE.

NANCY LOU DEEDS, 14-YEAR-OLD PIANIST TO MAKE CONCERT STAGE DEBUT ON MARCH 11.

AKRON GIRL TO MAKE STAGE DEBUT ON TV.

AKRON GIRL ORCHESTRA SOLOIST "STAGE FRIGHT? WHAT'S THAT?"

The invincibility of American youth is to be demonstrated again Thursday night when pretty, 14-year-old Nancy Lou Deeds of Akron, Colorado steps onto the stage of Phipps Auditorium. Nancy Lou will be making her debut as piano

soloist with the Denver Businessmen's orchestra ... ...
she isn't the least bit nervous over the approaching
concert. True to the tradition of American youth who will
dare anything, she doesn't see anything to be frightened
about. Besides, Dr. Brico will be on the podium.

Alex Murphree, *Denver Post* Drama Editor
March 9, 1954

B is not only an inspiring and demanding teacher, she
is also a talented and tireless promoter. Articles in
some of the local papers appeared as early as July
1953, but by January 1954, B had generated enough
interest to secure for herself and her protégée, several
television appearances – most of them announced in
The Denver Post Playbills and some in my diary:

FRIDAY AFTERNOON, 3:30 PM
EDDIE ROGERS SHOW GUEST, 14-YEAR-OLD
PIANIST, NANCY LOU DEEDS.

WEDNESDAY EVENING, 7:30 PM
RAY PERKINS SHOW GUEST, 14-YEAR-OLD
PIANIST NANCY LOU DEEDS.

FRIDAY AFTERNOON, 3:30 PM
DALE MORGAN SHOW INTERVIEW WITH
CONDUCTOR DR. A B AND HER PROTÉGÉE,
14-YEAR-OLD PIANIST NANCY LOU DEEDS.

*Dear Diary, This afternoon I was on TV again, the
Eddie Rogers Show. I played "Gnomes" from Pictures At
An Exhibition ... everyone complimented me. Sure be
glad to get back home, though.*

Dear Diary, More TV shows. Today I was on the Ray Perkins Show.

Mother and Daddy got to hear orchestral rehearsal tonight. It went real good.

March 3

Today we went to the TV studios again. Dale Morgan recorded an interview with Dr. Brico for his show tomorrow. I played "The Gates of Kiev" from Pictures. TV sure is fun.

March 4

Was on the June Sterling TV show today. Practiced. LL called, wanted to take me to a movie. Ugh. I said I was busy.

March 5

O n the morning of March 11, the day of my debut, skies over the snow-capped Rockies darken and a deeper chill bites into the bones. I, the young protégée, rest and am treated to a fine lunch at the Tiffin Inn by Margaret Davis, great-granddaughter of Governor Evans, Colorado's first governor and B's closest friend. One-half of a perfectly roasted chicken with a side of steamed vegetables is ordered for me, who has only ever eaten my mother's delicious fried chicken. So I am instructed by B on carving the meat from the bone with utensils. A good deal of chicken clings to the carcass when I am finished.

Silence and complete rest are prescribed for the afternoon. Calming myself by softly singing one or two stanzas from a handful of country and western tunes I have ingrained somewhere (I thought many years later) in my reptilian brain.

By evening, the storm which Weatherman Bowman predicted for the following morning, has moved in, and by the time B and I head for Phipps Auditorium, the streets are already slick and wet, and snow layering itself poetically onto the thick brush of pines, so that the driver is forced to nose the car forward ever more slowly through the thick curtain of falling white flakes. To me, the myopic child, it is as if we are tunneling our way into the center of a revolving kaleidoscope.

In spite of the weather hazards, the car reaches the auditorium in plenty of time and the small entourage disembarks and heads backstage to still nerves and warm up cold fingers. Soon there is applause as B, bosom thrust forward and head thrust up and back, sweeps onto stage and mounts the podium. The click of her baton, strains of Gluck's *Overture Iphigenia in Aulis*.

It has begun.

*S*uddenly it is over. The orchestra rises, clapping; the concertmaster stands, clapping vigorously, his violin tucked under his right arm; a few stentorian "bravos" are heard rising out of the audience, all clapping; young girls run down the aisles carrying bouquets of roses.

The young performer stands.

Although I am smiling, I feel more dazed than

transported.

*Y*ears later, I remember only this: I remember walking onstage; I remember bowing and worrying that the bodice of my strapless gown might slip to indecent levels; I remember the orchestra's pride and pleasure, B's presence; the audience clapping, cries of "bravo"; I remember the young women and their gifts of flowers.

I remember the ice cream party at Bauer's afterwards.

But I don't remember playing a single note.

*L*ater, in the silence and darkness of that night, a form of awakening washes through me – a kind of immense satisfaction, pleasure at all I have accomplished. It feels as though I have been specially selected for great things – have been touched, filled with the essence of God.

Disturbances of the Inner Ear

The Myth of Genius

It was Antonia's first concert of her New York Women's Symphony ... ... she conducted marvelously – a demon, a force, a compelling performance – all Carnegie Hall electrified.

Anaïs Nin, Diary entry, March 11, 1934

I can't express all of my feelings on this great day. I am happy, confused and excited. I only hope that this turns out to be the beginning. Dr. Brico was very pleased with me. She is positively the most wonderful person I have ever known. Mrs. Davis had a party for me at Bauer's. If the weather hadn't been so bad, more from outside Denver would have attended. I got three bouquets of roses – pink, red, and yellow – one from the orchestra, Mother and Daddy, and the people in Baca County. I got several curtain calls. The orchestra was as proud as anyone. I know now, as I have realized many times recently, that this is the only life for me. I only hope God will give me patience, courage, and faith. I feel it was a wonderful debut.

Nancy Lou Deeds, Diary entry, March 11, 1954

DENVER POST

March 12, 1954

The frequency with which cold weather coincides with concerts by the Denver Businessmen's Orchestra at Phipps Auditorium has become more and more meaningless because of the sincerity and sense of accomplishment their concerts regularly establish ... ...

To coin a phrase, Miss Deeds went to town with the Mozart. She played admirably, cleanly, and sympathetically, showing grace in runs and projecting a nice feeling for the beauties of the Mozart Concerto in A Major K 488, the concerto of the evening.

The assurance of her playing which enhanced the performance was no false or immodest one, nor was her playing based on any assumptions that would lead her astray. It was direct, uncomplicated and careful ... ...

Greater strength would have given her more assurance in the final measures and also another quality, which will come with experience and age, the ability to tie together the widely separated notes of an andante ... ...

Allen Young,

Dearest Nancy,

Soon it will be your birthday! You will be all of 15 years old!! And you have the world and all it offers before you! It is far to unlock the gates to further musical treasures and the joy of achievement that it brings with it. Remain true to your inner musical self and be sure that I will guide and help you along the way to the best of my ability and with a heart full of love and complete confidence! This is only a short message to you. I couldn't possibly put on paper all I feel in my heart, nor could I say how very proud I was of your dedication to your task. Keep ever the ideal of perfection before you and remain humble! And you will have countless joys musical, spiritual, and material.

46

Much love, your friend and teacher,

Tante Antonia

Birthday card from Dr. Brico, March 12, 1954

MANCHESTER GUARDIAN

1992

In 1956, pianist György Cziffra was hailed as a diabolical protégé, a reincarnation of Liszt. Twenty years later, the influential Paris radio station, a Trabine des Critiques de Disques, said after hearing Cziffra's version of Liszt's Les Anne's di Pilerinage: when you play like that there is only one thing left for you to do and that's commit suicide.

*W*hat resonates here among these fragmented facts and imaginings? What thread runs through these excerpts? B's triumphant March 11,1934 conducting debut as recorded by Anaïs Nin? My own musical debut with B's Denver Symphony Orchestra on March 11, 1954; the strong passions it inspires in me and that I pour into my diary later that same night? Allen Young's *Denver Post* review of that concert, B's birthday message and, forty years later, the triangulating force: the esthetic assassination of pianist György Cziffra?

It is the devastating message about Cziffra that sends me flying back, digging through shadows and scraps of paper for evidence of *my* assassination – evidence, a *reason* to explain my own musical suicide.

What I find dispirits me, but forces me on: Allen Young's neck bone of "praise":

… she played admirably, cleanly, sympathetically … … …
an inability to tie together the widely separated notes of an

andante …
   and
… a weakness in the final measures …

No mention here of "exceptional talent," of "genius." No, far from it. Then, B's birthday message of encouragement and future expectation, her pride in my "dedication to my task." Yes, but no mention of "genius" certainly; not even of a *brilliance* in my performance.

With each dig for evidence and each artifact uncovered, my "need to know" reasserts itself, grows in urgency; each time, gathering gravitas, demanding resolution. Every fresh find seems only to deepen the mystery. And who was any longer among the living who might throw light on this decades-old event?

A dream, perhaps, reminds me of a reel-to-reel recording of my March 11 concert. I spring up again, hauling boxes and files and garment bags out of closets in a frantic attempt to locate the irrefutable evidence of my success. Or of my failure.

To understand what the tape reveals when I find it, you need certain other information. In the mid-1970s, I underwent life-threatening surgery. It left my system drained and my body, especially my eyes, always weak and easily strained, depleted. For six weeks after surgery, I sat about in the dark, my eyes unable to allow even thin slants of light into the room, reading an impossibility. At this time I discovered "Tapes for the Blind." Their catalog of titles is impressive and the tapes may be borrowed free of charge for qualified individuals, of which I was temporarily one.

The tapes, when they arrived, were grossly inadequate, read by convicts who were not up to the task of reading Hesse or Dostoevsky. Although far from the intellectual inspiration I had expected, the tapes provided a distraction for which I was grateful. I had forgotten, in fact, that on one or two occasions, I made a duplicate tape of an entire book, believing I would want to return to it at some future date. As my body restored itself, my eyes grew stronger again. I returned all of the borrowed tapes and, feeling a well of gratitude, again, took up my reading.

And so, in an almost biblical sense, it has come to pass that twenty-seven years later, I am to remember with great force those weeks of recovery and darkness, and the rough voices of convicts. A memory that might have lain submerged but for my drivenness to locate this historical record of my debut.

The black and red Scotch Tape box, when I find it, hides at the back of a linen closet in the company of several smaller unboxed reels of home movies. Triumphant, I hug the box to me and make immediate plans to deliver the tape to the city where its contents can be transferred to a format I can play on my modern audio equipment. For nearly a week, anxiety stalks me. What will the tape reveal? Brilliance or dismal failure? Glowing success or shameful humiliation? I hope for the first, but fear the second.

The revelation, when it comes, is unexpected and dismally disappointing: not a single note is audible on

49

the coiled length of the two-hour tape. What is complete and completely audible, however, is the deep, stumbling voice of Butch reading the entire text of Dostoevsky's *The Idiot.*

Beyond Applause

*Your music echoes under the beams
in Cherry Hall. Thank you for it.*
~ Jeanne Cherry
(Carmel, July 31, 1954)

*A*n unknown woman, slight and gray, steps out
of the blur of the audience and hands me a gift.
It is a sterling silver bracelet in the shape of
a musical measure, complete with staff, notes, and three
jubilant musicians. It is defined by its unusual aspect,
the importance of its weight, the surprise of its gift.
Although it was July, I remember this mysterious
woman bundled in tweed coat and knitted hat. Perhaps
this is right, for Carmel summer evenings are most often
enveloped in chill and descending gray fog that always
reminds me of pewter. Along with fragments of a
porcelain and signed Delft pendant brought to me from
Holland by my teacher, Antonia Brico, this bracelet is
the only other material remnant remaining from those
musical years.

It is 1954 and I am fresh from my debut with The
Denver Businessmen's Symphony, an orchestra Dr.
Brico conducted for 40 years. As both reward and

inspiration, Brico and her close friend, Margaret Davis, conspire to bestow upon me this journey out of rural Colorado into the cultural milieu of California. Family fortunes could not support such a trip. Mrs. Davis sends two letters, the first to my parents, the second to me.

Mrs. Roblin H. Davis
Evans Ranch
Evergreen, Colorado

Dear Mrs. Deeds.

Will you please read the enclosed note to Nancy. If you and Mr. Deeds really want her to go with Dr. Brico, and will let me do this, I shall be very happy indeed. I owe a very great deal to Dr. Brico, and, knowing what a joy it would be for her to have Nancy with her, feel that in this way I may perhaps be repaying her in a small way as well as giving myself the pleasure of sharing an adventure with Nancy.

But if, for any reason, you do not approve or wish this trip for Nancy, I shall quite understand and hope that, then, you will say nothing about it to the child but simply return my note to her and cheque.

With very best wishes to you both,

Very sincerely,
Margaret Davis
1310 Bannock St.
May 12 1954

By this time, my parents have already sacrificed a great deal during the past four years to finance my musical career and so surely feel a large measure of relief at receiving Mrs. Davis's offer. Still, it is a difficult decision. Their commitment to supporting and furthering my opportunities for a career as a concert pianist against their consternation at the prospect of such a journey to a state they themselves had never seen.

I could only appreciate their dilemma after mothering two daughters of my own.

Mrs. Davis's letter to me included a $200 check and read:

Mrs. Roblin H. Davis
Evans Ranch
Evergreen, Colorado
May 12, 1954

Dear Nancy;

I can think of nothing more wonderful than to see Carmel and the Pacific Ocean with Dr. Brico. Now, I cannot go myself, but perhaps you can go for me, and I shall have the double joy of knowing you are helping her as well as having a real adventure yourself.

You will make me very happy if you can do this, and will accept the enclosed cheque.

Love from Mrs. Davis

And so I train to California, to Carmel, and to the small concert stage of the Cherry Foundation, which sponsors various cultural events, everything from Punch and Judy puppet shows to lectures and recitals. I am paid $50 for my recital; Brico is paid to lecture. This summer she talks about her visits to Albert Schweitzer in Lamborene, Africa. Listening to the tape of it years later, the so-familiar voice, its inflections, its honeyed tones, all rush back as though it happened only last

53

summer. And yet, no real memory of this comes and I wonder how it is possible that I have forgotten.

The performance hall at the Carl Cherry Foundation seats perhaps 125. The floors are all polished hardwood and a small kind of stage wraps itself around one end of the room. The *Pinecone* records that I performed the Brahms *Rhapsody In B Flat* and the Paderewski *Coccovienne*. The seats are all filled as the local papers have carried news of the event in advance of our coming. The unknown woman bearing her gift is one of those present.

Madame Cherry, or Jeanne D'Orge as she is known in the art word, founded the Cherry Foundation in 1948 after her husband's death. Carl Cherry, an inventor, made his money on his invention of a rivet that added safety, speed, and thrift to assembling parts on airplanes, especially valuable during the final years of World War II.

Draped in layers of long Oriental sorts of dress and shawls interwoven with iridescent threads and yarns. Limp and colorless hair frames her broadly soft face, which exactly matches her rounded physique. But in spite of so much softness, she exudes a quality of substance and "otherness" that awe and intimidate me.

Madame Cherry, or Jeanne D'Orge, is known and respected not only for her work in the Foundation, but too for her paintings, abstracts of color and textures unlike anything I have seen. Unlike my father's oil landscape paintings covering the walls of our home, which are beautiful pastoral or mountain scenes in tones of spring and summer greens or soft, comforting blues.

Jeanne D'Orge's work, swipes and waves of strong colors, bright and dark, suggests another mind, another consciousness. Dr. Brico impresses upon me this woman's singularity and ingenuity, relating how during the war when materials were scarce, Jeanne painted on whatever she had on hand, scraps of cardboard, cookie sheets.

(Madame Cherry wafts through my memory, manifesting and dematerializing like a phantom, a shapeless and unfashionable figure. Jeanne D'Orge gave me one of her darker works, hanging now in my room. The painting is a part of my life with its dark abstractions of mountains and valleys and other-worldly streams.)

When Dr. Brico intercedes on my behalf, it is certain that her efforts on her own behalf are greater. If she procures one painting for me, she invariably secures half a dozen for herself. Her habit and manner of wheedling and begging original art from every artist we visit, presents a side of her I find embarrassing and demeaning.

Lately, rediscovering the Cherry Foundation, I learn that Jeanne D'Orge was a poet in earlier life. She knew Marianne Moore, William Carlos Williams and Wallace Stevens. Whether D'Orge and Brico first met in Europe or New York, I can't say, but the Cherry Foundation is a constant in Brico's summer life. Of my performance there, my diary records that "I played very good, especially the Brahms *Rhapsody in B Flat* and the Paderewski *Croccovienne.* Very enthusiastic crowd. Had an egg on toast and ice cream. Mrs. Cherry gave me a painting. Went to bed."

(The egg on toast and ice cream meal I don't remember, although three-minute eggs, which I resist with stubbornness and horror, and ice cream, which I never resist, were favored Brico fare.)

More memorable is the meal served on our first night at the Foundation, with a long, austere table, long enough to afford seating for at least fifty people, I think now, but barely imaginable then. The menu is even more unimaginable. I recoil at the entrée passed to me by the woman on my left. Something about the shape of the meat looks repulsive and vulgar. The woman tells me that it is boiled tongue. "A delicacy," she says, encouraging me. The image of this swollen part resting on its oversized platter of parsley is unforgettable. It makes me think of a male organ, although I don't know what one looks like. Brico cuts me a piece and urges me to take a bite of it, but I hide it under fragments of roasted vegetables and manage never to taste it.

A special quality marks my memories of Carmel-by-the-Sea and the Cherry Foundation. In 1954, I feel, as my father counseled, "I have hitched my chariot to a star," and set a course to forever live among the constellations. Much later I see that, already that summer my star is turning retrograde and that my chariot moves steadily towards re-entry into the stormy atmospheres of planet earth.

Holy Mountain and the Women of Lunar Lights

*H*ere they are, the cluster of women in their swimsuits, sitting on the sands of Mt. Washington. The young, redheaded beauty among them, pushing back a rush of hair with one hand – the rest round or angular, sitting serene as swamis – and at the rear of the group sits Brico, her sturdy body clothed in a two-piece black bathing suit, her head in a shower cap.

In the photograph (snapped with a Brownie box camera), the distinctive faces and figures of some of the women, which express a corner of personality, capture my attention. The tall, plain one is an artist who gives me a charcoal drawing, a dark still life of a scythe, a drape, and a wheel. I am drawn to the beautiful and mysterious redhead and feel that she vibrates with a worldly energy. I remember the stories of her life that include a foreign country, a Persian prince, adventures that end in deprivation and abuse. I want to know about the significance of the tri-metal, twisted bracelets she wears above each elbow. They match the ones that Brico wears above her elbows. Twisted strands of silver, gold, and copper, the end of one tipped with turquoise, the other with coral.

At some point, I notice the small dark child who sits alone at the edge of the frame. Her small shoulders droop and she has a cast on her right arm. She looks into the camera with dark, sad eyes. It is Ingrid. She is Swiss and brought to this country by Brico, who would like to adopt her. Intimations of this intent are kept from Ingrid, who, it seems clear to me, would much prefer to return to Switzerland to be with her own parents.

This is a curious and ill-assorted group, looking, I think, like a group of vacationing women having a pleasant afternoon on the shore.

In the penetralia of the temple in the background, there is apparently a holy man and the room is filled with his prayers. When the women retreat at last into the temple, the hissing of their whispers disturbs the air. I wait with Ingrid outside. We are not among those allowed entry into the sacred inner space, but a few of the whispered words – *master, he, how long?* – escape and linger in the air.

I try to put Ingrid out of my mind. I want to forget her presence, now and later when we spend a long week at Harbon Hot Springs. Brico has instructed her to spend the week teaching me German. I want Ingrid to return to Switzerland. I feel that Ingrid, this frail and innocent child, is usurping my place in my teacher's heart. Later, I manage to repress the fact of Ingrid's presence that summer until I come upon the photograph of Ingrid sitting among the group of women.

But I know that I will remember the women always, those monastic disciples, and how, in the arch of the temple, they stood together in attitudes of sorrow and anticipation, as though waiting for a resurrection, while grieving a yet unresolved death.

Ingrid and I Refuse the Waters

Dear Diary, This morning Mrs. Johnsten drove us to Berkeley and we had lunch, then rode with friends to Harbin Hot Springs. Went in swimming before and after supper. Dr. Brico wants Ingrid to teach me German. Today I learned to say, Sprechen sie Deutsch?

~ August 1, 1954

Dear Diary, Today we sunbathed and went swimming all day. I learned to float. Dr. Brico got mad at me because I went into the fenced area with my swimsuit on. She was lying on a wooden bench and she didn't have a swimsuit on. She sure was mad! I got a letter from home today. Sure glad to hear from them. Wish we were going home sooner.

~August 3, 1954

I am tired of swimming and trying to teach the American girl my language like Tante Tonia wants me to. The American girl does not want to learn my language, she does not like me much, I think. She wants to sit by the pool alone and write in her little book. So much she wants to be alone. Always alone. I think she writes secrets. Maybe she writes how she doesn't like me. Maybe she writes about Tante Tonia. Soon Tante Tonia will ask her again to see her little book with its secrets. But she will not show her book to Tante Tonia.

Dear Diary, Today we went swimming and sunbathed again. There is nothing else to do here. This afternoon we drove to another resort and they had an outside dance floor and colored paper lanterns and young people sitting on the grass talking. It sure looked like fun. I wish we were staying there. Dr. Brico didn't like it though.

Tonight I played for people in the lobby and they recorded the Beethoven 32 Variations. A man wrote in my autograph book: "I heard Nancy play a few piano numbers today and they were so beautifully done, even tho' one key did not function. In the future, I shall hear a finished artist." He was nice.

~ August 4, 1954

Again today the American girl sits by the pool writing. Alone. Tante Tonia is in that dark little room at the top of those stairs sitting in the die große Badewanne. I don't want to go in there. It is dark and the air is full of hot water and Tante Tonia does not wear any clothes. It scares me. The American girl will not go there either.

There is nothing to do and I am tired of swimming. The American girl cannot swim. She sinks. I tried to teach her to dive, but she is afraid of sinking. She does not want me to teach her.

Tante Tonia loves it here. I love it not. The American girl loves it not. It is a place for alte Menschen. I am not old. The American girl is not old. My heart hurts for my parents and I want to go home. I do not want to live with Tante Tonia. The American girl wants to go home. We are both happy at home.

Harbin Hot Springs
August 5, 1954

Dearest Gaylord,

The time here has been good for me, but it is almost over. The baths have done wonders for my "conducting" arm and shoulder just as you said they would. You know how anxious I was about them! I carry your *Treasure of Secrets* everywhere, as you know. Lela Booth's cook here at Harbin caters to me, making your "sun butter" and keeping a supply of your vegetable salt. Your chapter "Fight Fatigue with Relaxation and Exercise" has been invaluable, also. I recently read another article, "Gayelord Hauser Invents the Celebrity Diet" and about how many Hollywood stars you have "converted." It pleases me to know things are going so well for you.

I arrived here still very tired from the opera business, but have been faithful to your regimen – the hot springs, lemon water, and the air baths. I am having a grand rest, but, of course, Lela has been tempting me to a teeny bit of excess with such fine food. I have not, alas, been completely faithful to your diet regime and my profile seems to have increased slightly since arriving. (I check it in the mirror in my room every morning before going to the lodge for breakfast!) I am constant in Master's recharging exercises, though, and they restore me – a great benefit. I miss Master so terribly. He will continue to influence and direct my life, as you already know.

The little child, Ingrid, my "adopted daughter" and Nancy, my young piano protégée, are becoming friends here. We are having a marvelous time and it is unfortunate that we must leave tomorrow. We will tour north for one day, then return to San Francisco on Thursday.

Why haven't you written? I am so disappointed at not getting to see you while I am in California. PLEASE write to me as you promised! At least a postcard!!!

Much love,

Antonia

Dear Diary, We go to San Francisco tomorrow. I love San Francisco and want to live there. Dr. Brico says I have to live in Carmel because that is where she is buying a house, but I want to live in San Francisco. We'll stay with Lorraine and Winifred. Sure will be glad to get home!

Today we went swimming again and then left for the Redwood hiway. Slept in motel in Willets. Went to show. "Riders to the Stars" very good.

~ August 6, 1954

Dear Diary, Today we went up the Redwood hiway, bought souvenirs. Slept in a motel on way back. Redwoods very pretty. Saw Tree House.

~August 7, 1954

Motor Lodge Murder

J am at a holiday lodge of some sort with friends and a girl we know is found murdered, drowned in the ocean. She had been to a particular motor lodge restroom or restaurant prior and we talk of the bad vibes surrounding the place. Then I am lounging on a pad in the back of a pick-up before the festivities and a girl comes and demands her "place back" as though I had taken it and says she can prove it is hers as she left some stuff under the pillow. I say I don't need proof. I just didn't realize space was taken. I leave not feeling any guilt or shame.

Then I discover Brico has handwritten me into the evening program to play Brahms and another piece. At first, I can't figure out who did it, then I recognize her writing. The piano is terrible, it looks good, but the keys are stiff and will hardly depress. I realize that there is no way I can or will perform! I discuss it with a friend how to handle it – go around cutting my portion off the programs? Write a note to the person in charge? I don't find anyone in charge. I can't wait for them to call on me and then be embarrassed in front of my friends. I can't decide what to do. As other friends arrive, and as we sit around the motor lodge, we talk about it being the place that held bad vibes for the murdered girl. I think that the omens it holds for me are good since this is the second opportunity I have had on this day to perform as a pianist. While I worry about how to cancel my performance, I realize that people will not have a full evening's entertainment if I don't perform. I figure how much time the pieces I am to play will take, the Brahms about 15 minutes. Pondering this new problem, I glance at the well-dressed audience through the large glass windows. The room is brightly lit and the concert has begun, but no sound is audible. As I look in, however, the standing congregation lift their filled wine glasses in unison in a toast to the evening.

Sempre Con Fuoco

After our soiree north to Willets and the Redwood Tree House, we settle into Lorenne and Winifred's San Francisco flat for the last few days of our trip.

Concealing travel weariness and acute homesickness, I sit eating Winifred's fresh tossed greens and a hunk of sourdough loaf, fattening, almost, on its rich pungency. The women chatter and, occasionally, laugh in an off-color way at something one or the other says in a language I don't know, making me feel a child and invisible.

After the meal and conversation come to an end, I am asked to perform. This is a regular part of every evening that we spend in California that summer. This particular evening remains memorable, not for what I played – possibly the Beethoven 32 Variations, surely the Paderewski *Cracovienne* – but for my dark introduction to pianist William Kapell.

As I strike the final *Cracovienne* chord, applause breaks through the fading strains. Lorenne puts her fingers to her mouth and gives a shrill whistle before turning to Brico. This kid can *play*," she cries.

"Bravo!" she says to me.

"O yes, bravo, bravo! " Winifred echoes, leaning forward in her chair and clasping her small hands together. "Your touch reminds me so much of Willie Kapell. That passion, the same feeling of wild poetic fire."

"Ah, Kapell," Brico sighs. "A consummate musician. A genius. And what dedication to the work. One of the great pianists of this century."

"Winnie and I heard Kapell play in New York," Lorraine says, leaning back and putting her feet up on the chair's matching hassock. "Mussorgsky's *Pictures At An Exhibition*, Liszt's *Mephisto Waltz*. He was a fireball. What a performance!"

"Oh, it was unforgettable," says Winnie. "I've never heard anyone play the Liszt with such beautiful ferocity."

"Yes," Brico agrees. "*Sempre con fuoco*! An extraordinary talent, a passionate musician. He was a giant among pianists. Rubinstein, Fleicher, even Horowitz finally played in his shadow."

"He had just turned 31 when his plane went down just three minutes out of San Francisco," Lorenne says. "He was returning from a concert in Australia. God, to think of it!"

"He was so young," breathes Winifred.

"But," Brico says, "is it not so often this way, that the special talents are given only a measure of time on this earth. Theirs must be an urgency of purpose. Their gifts and the practice above everything else!"

She shoots me her gaze. It catches and holds me. I shudder.

Time-trussed, my life, I think, book-ended between Mozart's early death by disease and Kapell's sudden violent one. In between, looms death by cancer or death from the blast of an atomic bomb. At fifteen, dying begins to feel more palpable, more probable than living. I have already used up half of what will obviously be a short life! I begin to feel a free-floating anxiety and dread, coupled with a sense of near-hysterical urgency and purpose.

Two weeks later, back in Denver, Brico sits at the Steinway playing fragments of my new repertoire. She plays with great flourish and élan, dropping in extra notes, I suspect, for dramatic emphasis.

Each year, it is the same. Late summer, before she leaves for Europe, we meet and she discloses her plan for me in the coming year. It is a time of the greatest anticipation and excitement for me, not only because it means new, beautiful, and demanding work, but also because it signals a beginning, fresh possibilities. And, for a time afterwards, my spirits soar above shadows of darkness and death. There is only an attunement to the work and a commitment to the beauty and transcendence of the music.

At the end of this lesson, Brico takes up her pen and scrawls in the beige steno pad that is my lesson book, the new manuscripts I am to order from Patelson's Music Store in New York.

Prominent among this list is Mussorgsky's *Pictures At An Exhibition*. Also on the list is *Mephisto Waltz*, by Franz Liszt. My new concerto is in a minor key and composed by Schumann. It is as well that I do not know the story of his life at this time. All the same, I can see it now as symbolic in the way that the melody of my life has already begun transcribing out of a major and into a minor key.

A Rose, A Stone and an Urn

*J*inny sits on the large river stone near the gate, waving, her blonde hair gleams and her Norwegian accent drums through my head – the way her tongue turns *y* into *j*.

We have come to visit Jinny and George Steiner. I have the sense that they are not particular friends of B's. George, B tells me, is a businessman, which makes the visit even more surprising. Later, I find that he is also an artist.

"Watch jour paintings!" Jinny cries as we load ourselves into the small car. Said only half in jest, having witnessed Brico's greed earlier in the evening. I remember this and hug the two unframed sketches close to my chest.

George stands in the door, his virile frame half hidden in shadow. Even with myopic vision, I can see, underlying his smile, the slight impatience to return to his pads, his pens, his inkpots.

I climb into the back seat of the old Plymouth behind Brico and Breva, our driver, glad to have at least this small separation, this little freedom. It is not yet dark and I steal a long look at the two drawings George has given me. One is a 3" x 5" sketch of Mozart, one of what George calls his "whimsies." It has been done all in a rush in black ink and has a gay and uninhibited quality to it. Befitting Mozart, I think.

The other drawing, the one Brico had hoped to wheedle for herself, is much larger, intricately imagined and skillfully implemented. A bespectacled scientist sits in his laboratory poring over a table jammed with bottles, Bunson burners, books and paraphernalia. The upper portion of the drawing overflows with the subject's thoughts, his visions, formulae, solutions. I hold the two original artworks and settle back in my seat. Jinny's feast earlier that evening has warmed and relaxed me and I doze off, blocking out the mischievous dialogue of the two women in the front seat.

It is two years before I visit California and see Jinny again. And again it is with Brico. We arrive unannounced one Sunday afternoon to find Jinny alone. She greets us in a distracted manner, but smiles when she recognizes me and gives me a hug. She speaks in hushed tones, her face clouded and still.

She shows us into George's studio, now dimly lit. On his drawing board a dark red rose droops over the lip of a crystal vase, its petals lifeless and dark.

The air carries the smell of inactivity, disuse, and on the mantel there is a wooden urn. I had been to my grandmother's funeral, I had seen her body after life. I cannot imagine that in the urn rests a tiny mound of dust, all that is left of the human remains of Standard oil magnate and artist George Albert Schreiner, III.

On this last visit, we carry away with us no gifts of art. Only memories.

A Watershed Year

Dr. Antonia Brico
959 S. Pennsylvania
Denver 9, Colorado

Christmas Letter, 1954

Dearest Nancy,

The warmest of the Season's Greetings are sent to you, my dear friends all over the world with this, our third annual Christmas newsletter. So much has happened in the past year that it would require a magazine instead of a letter to give all the details.

To begin with, after twelve years of maintaining a studio, and an apartment around the corner, I decided to turn the monthly rent into payment on a house and SO in August, I bought a HOME!!! This one to live in since the Carmel, California, property is fortunately all paid for and will serve as an investment for the future. My new studio-residence is a two-story brick with plenty of room – basement, garage, glassed-in porch, a lovely studio, and yard and is located in a nice residential district. My entire Beethoven collection, which has grown considerably, is now in the main studio, which we call Beethoven Hall.

Surprise number two — since Easter I have had as a guest a little Swiss child, Ingrid, age 11 (now 12), whom I met while in Switzerland. She is musically very gifted and so I am educating her in every way possible. Her parents, who are at the moment in Toronto, Canada, will subsequently come to Denver to live.

Artistically very much has happened including the formation of the Greater Denver Opera Association of which I am one of the conductors — directing the opening performances of "Pagliacci" and "Gianni Schicchi" in March, 1954. On February 16, 17, and 18, 1955, I shall conduct the delightful opera, "Hansel and Gretel" by Humperdinck and in October, Puccini's "La Boehme". A longing of many years was satisfied when the Businessmen's Symphony, under my direction, presented a concert version of Beethoven's only opera "Fidelio", in May, 1954.

As usual, I went to Europe via California taking with me Nancy Lou Deeds, a very gifted fifteen-year-old pianist (who played the Mozart Concerto with my Denver Businessmen's Symphony last March) and Ingrid. Nancy played her first out of state concert in Carmel, California, and I also gave a lecture thanks to the invitation of the Cherry Foundation. Mrs. Carl Cherry, President of the Foundation whose original and dynamic paintings attract visitors from all over the States, has her studio and a lovely concert hall in Carmel.

It is still difficult to settle down to earth after the dramatic, beautiful, and artistically satisfying experiences in Europe. Although my stay was considerably shorter this year, it was very intense. I flew over and back with KIM Airlines and was on the

Continent from the 29th of September to the 12th of November. Upon landing in Amsterdam I entrained immediately for the Alsace-Lorraine and the little village of Guns Bach to visit and study with, once more, Dr. Albert Schweitzer, who was at that moment preparing his acceptance speech for the Nobel Prize which was awarded to him November 4th.

It is five years since this great man first came to lecture at Aspen, Colorado, and I am truly grateful that the fates have permitted me this yearly pilgrimage and all that it has meant in the way of education and inspiration be it in France or Africa.

Although I visited friends in Paris, Switzerland, Austria, and Germany, I spent every possible moment studying the scores for the two concerts which I conducted in Brussels, Belgium, November 7 and Amsterdam, Holland, November 11th. The first was a command performance arranged for me by Her Majesty, the Dowager Queen Elizabeth of Belgium, whom I had the honor to meet at Dr. Schweitzer's home two years previous.

Everyone must try to read between the lines to appreciate the beauty and wonder of the six days I spent as the guest of Her Majesty at the Chateau Royal de Stuyvenberg (the Queen's Palace). The Queen's chauffeur drove me to orchestra rehearsals and press conferences – the rest of the time was spent in study and playing chamber music with Her Majesty the Queen, who is a fine violinist. The highlight of the week, of course, was the concert which the Queen attended ... There was a large enthusiastic invitational audience as well as a radio broadcast.

From Brussels I went to Amsterdam to conduct the

Netherlands Radio symphony in a program of "Tristan Prelude" and "Love-Death" by Wagner, Stravinsky's "Firebird Suite," and Sibelius' "Seventh Symphony." Both orchestras were of the highest caliber, comparable only to Toscanini's NBC or the Boston Symphony. In both countries, the American press and cultural attaché was very very cooperative and helpful. Both arranged press conferences and furnished news releases to the American colony in the two cities.

For the first time since my yearly visit to Europe, I was unable to go to Finland. However, Professor Sibelius, who is now eighty-nine years young, heard my Amsterdam concert on the radio and was very pleased with it.

Immediately following my Amsterdam concert I flew back to the States and home where rehearsals were already in progress under the direction of my capable assistant conductor Karlos Moser who was my protégé and my most gifted student in piano and conducting from the time he was eleven years of age until he entered Princeton. He has now returned with his lovely singer-pianist wife, Arconia.

Much love

Tante Antonia

Through a Dark Wood

Inheriting the Wind

Dear Diary,

We sold our ranch here. We're going to have to move back to Pritchett, I guess.

January 20, 1954
Akron, Colorado

Dear Diary,

Daddy called me at school from Pritchett. Can't come home because of blowing snow and dust storms.

March 16, 1954

Dear Diary,

Today about noon we pulled out to move back to Pritchett. Daddy and Eddy in the truck. We ate in Akron, ate supper in Lamar. Got in about 9:30 pm.

May 25, 1954

Today we cleaned the house. Was it ever a mess! Dirt so deep we almost had to shovel it out. So tired tonight I could drop.

I hate this wind!

May 26, 1954

Pritchett, Colorado, located in Baca County, claims 738.43 miles of land area and .03 miles of water area. During the Dust Bowl years of the 1950s, severe drought and blowing winds reduced even this .03 area of water miles to less, turning this and surrounding counties of the plains of southeastern Colorado into a dark and sterile desert.

Roiling clouds of dust sweep across the land, sometimes in swirling vertical columns and sometimes in dense acres-wide horizontal clouds of darkness. Topsoil from pastures, farmlands and cemeteries is caught up in the malignity of the idiot wind and blown into eyes and up nostrils; blown through cracks of windows and doors and settling on table tops and over floors. Every surface and open human orifice becomes a kind of reliquary.

It is to this, on August 18, 1954, that we return.

Molto Aggitato

DENVER 1955.

The glassed-in porch at the rear of Tante Antonia's new house at 959 South Pennsylvania is closed off from the rest of the house and unheated. At 4:30 a.m. on a January morning, the thick layer of bedclothes fails to defend against bone-chilling mid-winter blasts of freezing air driving its way through the old ill-fitting windows. I pull the blankets higher over my head, breathing in slightly warmer air, undercover.

From the large studio on the other side of the house, Tante, a tray of stewed and fresh fruit on a small table beside her, sits practicing Rachmaninoff's Third Piano Concerto. In-between snatches of daydreaming, I see her large hands, smooth-skinned and handsome, mapped with purple veins that seem to tumesce whenever she plays. Again and again, the same terrible cadences. I know them all by heart. The devil Rachmaninoff, with his exposed emotions, his treacherous passages - his measures of seraphic sweetness.

How Tante exalts the music! Never one to be deflected from her course by difficulty or fear, she approaches Rachmaninoff's Third as she approaches the rest of life: with that combination of Dutch determination and Italian passion that is her heritage. The playing, however lacking in minor technical aspects, displays a certain precision and muscular brilliance, the whole of which fills me. Her first obsession and lasting love has ever been the piano, regardless of what she has fed the press; conducting, always, only the consolation.

When at last a faint metallic light threads its way through the icy film on the small high windows above where I listen and dream, I manage to rouse my slothful and recalcitrant body and reconcile myself to facing another unpromising day. My own practice is going poorly, the heart somehow excised from the dream – or perhaps buried in it. I, most of all, barely recognize the problem and I, least of all, have any solution.

By the time I bundle myself into my woolen and plaid Pendleton skirt and matching sweater set, both stiff with chill, it is nearly 8:00 o'clock. Tante's first student will be coming in less than an hour. I quicken my pace in order to gain an hour of solitary time in the kitchen over my toast and tea.

Pulling two pieces of wheat bread from the breadbox, I plug in the old manual toaster. This relic, a holdover from the 1940s, seems to have some mysterious significance for Tante, or perhaps it is just one more measure of her innate frugality, but I hate the thing. Teardrop slits perforate each of its twin, hinged doors. I plop the bread into their slots, careful to avoid touching the red glow of the strangulated wires burning with, I think, a dull passion of their own.

Sitting slumped on the bench near the counter, warmed by the red eye of the toaster and mesmerized in part by the particularly difficult *ossia* in the third movement that Tante now repeatedly attacks with vigor, I am startled from my reveries by smoke roiling from all sides of the ancient appliance.

Patterns of charcoal form, smudging the thickening air a cyanotic gray. I yank the electric cord from its socket; the tangled pattern of blistering wires glare their ferocious heat in electrifying condemnation of my inattention.

Suddenly a silence as dense as the charred air; as suffocating as a ponderous bosom. The rhythms of Rachmaninoff are replaced by the agitated, purposeful steps of Tante as she strides towards the kitchen entry. I back against the counter, bracing myself for the wind of her fury.

The door opens and the bulk of her sturdy, but voluptuous form materializes, dimly outlined through the dark and troubled air. Out of the shadow, the blade of her stern, angry voice. A reprimand.

The tape breaks here.

A splicing.

Slamming the door shut, she stomps back to her own pure tray of fruit, her Steinway, her Rachmaninoff.

I stand still, breathing in the stench of ash, my eyes watering from the thick, bruised air. Counterpointing emotions as complex as a fugue. I feel lumpen and humiliated, exiled and homesick, diminished by a deep sense of defect and shame. Throwing the cremains of the toast into the garbage, I tiptoe upstairs to the small bedroom where Franck's *Variations symphoniques* sits waiting on the old Steinway upright.

A Winter Lesson

I sit waiting, my gloved hands tucked into my armpits in an effort to bring feeling back into fingers numb and cold as icicles. I can see my breath as I exhale into the air, draw my limbs in closer to my body and breathe more shallowly, trying to recede into the Baroque pattern of the wallpaper.

The room is an exact 60 degrees, the temperature most beneficial for health. According to Europeans. According to Dr. Brico. Who is a European. It doesn't occur to me for forty years that it might have been an economical, rather than a health consideration. It would not have mattered to me, sitting there, bone-cold.

I feel colder now than I did walking the six blocks down Pennsylvania Avenue on snowy sidewalks in 34-degree weather to get here. I long for the warmth and comfort of my own home.

More often now I dream of Ken or Roger and not of Chopin or Mozart, but here, waiting, anxious and cold, warm romantic dreams vaporize and I find it easier to tune my mind to the frequency of the ongoing lesson.

It is not going well. The pupil has no talent and worse, has not practiced.

I look up, across the broad and glistening back of the magnificent Steinway and see the tight mouth and set jaw of the determined, but doomed child.

My pity for the child is tempered by the pity I expect to feel for myself in the next hour. The teacher's mood will not be a playful one. She will demand excellence and the intensity of her demand will affect my ability to produce it. Also, I have not practiced attentively, or enough, and my talent will not save me.

Brico, mind-reading it seems, turns. Her features relax a few degrees and she studies my face, fixes me with a burning and expectant gaze. For a moment. Then she screws her face into the terrible scowl of judgment and turns back to the child at the piano.

Soon, Brico taps her long and pointed baton on the shoulder of the instrument. One lesson is over. Another about to begin.

I think of running away. For a moment. Then I pick up my satchel and move toward the Steinway, stifling the scream of all I cannot or dare not articulate.

Brico Ponders, Finds a Solution

DENVER, JUNE 1956

*S*tudent recitals this summer have been more uneven than Brico can ever remember. A difficult year. Her two most senior students are moving off in directions she can fathom, but not control.

She sits late some nights meditating, wrapping their lives in her mantra: *Do not be deflected from your course.* She has laid glittering possibilities before them; on occasion, she has even wielded her baton more as a club than a magic wand. Entirely justified, she feels. Nothing so far has worked.

Anne, at least, has done well. If only some feeling came through - some heart. Her playing, so clean, hard-edged, so "scientific - so unencumbered by curves of desire or intimations of emotion. And how she sits at the instrument! In such furious concentration, her young female body stiff with a proud perfection. Perfect technique, but lacking some essential fire. Brico sighs. It was as though Anne solves algebraic equations even as her long and nimble fingers run unerringly through the Mendelssohn. Raised in a home with too much math and too little juice, Brico muses; well, she would doubtless succeed, but not as a performer.

And Carolyn. She works hard, has done a perfectly fine job on the Grieg. Its modest technical demands and Nordic heaviness suit her.

Brico gives every appearance of suddenly realizing just how tired she is of this concerto, and she sits calculating how many months and years Carolyn has been at it. But her calculations are obviously clouded by the image of Carolyn playing; shoulders hunched like a crow, her muscular shoulders heaving; her stubby fingers bludgeoning the keys. "Overdone," Brico pronounces. (And this is quite a pronouncement from someone who pulls out all of the dramatic stops, even when sight-reading with friends.)

A teacher is, however, complimented by a student's devoted labors and I perceive that Brico sees that a kind of blessedness arises out of Carolyn's perspiration and earnestness.

And Marianne, leaving for university. Stanley, too. And Danno, trading in the classical form to play jazz ensemble in Los Angeles. Why must they all leave?

Brico displays, though, that her most colossal failure of them all is Judy. Listening to Judy's careless and flawed playing of Rachmaninoff's Second at her last recital, a flippant performance, Brico radiates the loss of a life she had counted on to bring her own into greater celebrity. Here she has reckoned well, although it would be decades before Judy

Collins' and Jill Godmilows' film, *Portrait of a Woman*, gives Brico the national attention and fame I know she has craved her whole life.

Brico sighs as if in acknowledgment that she will have to let Judy go. Put up with studio whispers and gossip. As if she has seen it coming for months, has known that Judy, seduced by drugs and the music of blue guitars, is lost to her now – possibly forever.

But I see her eyes light on me, considering I might still be salvageable. So easily influenced, by Judy, by Charlotte, and until lately, by Brico herself. Nancy, emotional to the marrow; liquefying, merging into the Beethoven Sonata, the Chopin Ballade – *becoming* Schumann – adolescent emotions swelling, ironically counterpointing her discipline for the practice. Still, there is talent and a reservoir of deep feeling for the music.

There is that. Perhaps it is enough.

Nancy, her rising star, her fresh hope these last few years. But what of her now? It is a bad season for protégés. Yes, Nancy is her biggest challenge now. Late adolescence. Always a problem for girls. And the prettiness of her. This always gets in the way.

Brico looks down, perhaps reflecting on her own substantial European form: the heavy bosom, which gives her profile an almost unbalanced look; the prominent nose, the too-large, masculine face. "Prettiness" has never been an indictment leveled at her! She has never possessed even the shadow of a doll-like quality. And what are dolls for anyway? To play with! But maybe she thinks of this with sadness because dolls are also well loved.

For the moment of a measure, I feel Brico allow herself to grieve her unhappy and loveless childhood, her lost mother, the years of ill treatment by a malevolent and jealous stepmother.

However, being half Dutch and a practical individual, it is tangible how this old grief dissolves quickly into a fresh resolution for luring her problem protégée back into full fold.

She decides at last: competition and opportunity, that is the thing. She will take four of her top students with her to California where she is teaching concerto and opera seminars at the Music & Arts Institute. Anne and Carolyn, yes, certainly they deserve it, me, of course, and Charlotte? Well, why not. It could be arranged. She will speak bathetically with the parents, pull her long sad (some hinted "horsy") face, play up the opportunity. Even lay on a thin layer of guilt, if necessary. Her tactics seldom fail.

Yes, it could be arranged. Anne could play the Mendelssohn and Carolyn could do the Grieg *again* ... I almost hear Brico promising herself that this was positively the last time she would listen to Carolyn playing the Grief. I could play the Schumann - how hard, at first, she had practiced to work the expanse of Schumann into my small Mozartian hands. But Charlotte - the large, wrecked ballerina with her talent, her streaming red hair and her full mobile face. Well, Brico decides, the fourth will have to be Charlotte and she will have to play the Gershwin, the only piece in her repertoire and the only thing she seems remotely interested in playing. But she plays that well enough, Brico says. Plenty of juice there. And Charlotte clearly holds a fascination for Nancy. Charlotte has flair and a mystery that *is* appealing. But the "Rhapsody in Blue" in a concerto seminar? "Well, I will call it a concerto," Brico decides with her usual firmness.

Relieved at coming to what seemed a workable remedy for a troubling situation, Brico carries her cello over to the straight-back chair, props an orchestral score against the stand, and begins to lovingly wax her bow.

The cello, some say, is the most human of all musical instruments.

Chocolate Roulades and Hippo Burgers

July 1956, San Francisco

I sit on the steps reading the pamphlet she has picked up inside.

The Music & Arts Institute of San Francisco
is proud to have Dr. Antonia Brico giving summer
seminars in both piano and voice.
Dr. Brico has been acclaimed for her masterful
conducting of the foremost orchestras
throughout the world.

Concerto Repertoire
Master Class for Conductors, Soloists and Teachers
Coaching in Performance and Conducting of concerti for piano,
violin and all solo instruments with piano and available
ensemble.

Public performance. Etc.

Inquiries to: Director, Music and Arts Institute
2622 Jackson/Summer Session 1956
Fillmore 6-9748

The whole thing is disappointing. The Music & Arts Institute more resembles a mausoleum, I think, than the inspirational tabernacle I had expected. The cramped and windowless practice rooms, small as cells, with their dim yellow bulbs and dank gray walls!

But Carolyn sits stolidly in one of the airless rooms and continues to pound out the melodramatic Grieg. Next door, Anne's fingers gambol through the Mendelssohn, and down the hall, sometimes, Charlotte plays the *Rhapsody in Blue.*

As for myself, I play seldom and little. The topaz notes of Schumann die, stillborn in the close, crypt-like air. Feeling suffocated and blue (a mood I would in later years call "depressed"), I have no idea at all of how to revive Schumann, or, for that matter, myself.

Brico has secured four single rooms for us on the second floor of Mrs. Gepke's house at 1905 Pacific Avenue, half a dozen blocks from the Institute.

The four of us share the upstairs, which includes a bath and a kitchen, with a single boarder, a solemn middle-aged man. He is slim, slight in build, with a stern face that takes on a sour countenance as the summer wears on. He is elegant in black suit and black leather shoes, and he never goes out without his gloves, his black bowler, and his black walking stick.

He is, I think, romantically, an image of the city I love. He finds *us* unsophisticated, even distasteful.

"It's because we're sometimes loud," I tell

Charlotte, "and because we go out without hats and gloves."

Charlotte gives a toss of her lovely red head and sniffs. She can't be bothered to give the notion more attention than this. But I feel diminished by the boarder's aloofness and his disdain. It makes me feel, I think, "lowdown."

In-between practice sessions and lessons, we eat. Anne, her slice of rare roast beef red in its lukewarm juices; Carolyn her platter of spaghetti; and Charlotte and I, in addition to whatever else we eat, such as the monstrous burgers from the Hippopotamus down the hill on Van Ness, we eat mostly wedges of frozen chocolate and ice cream roulade. Our appetites seem only to increase with the feeding.

Charlotte's weight appears unchanged, hidden perhaps by her height and the ample yards of her polka-dot circular shirt. But by mid-summer, I have visibly ballooned. The waistband on my blue and gray dirndl skirt cuts into my flesh and the pearl buttons on my dark blouse strain against my flourishing bosom.

"Those roulades must be chock full of calories," I say to Charlotte, "and I am the body of empirical evidence."

"Nonsense," snorts Charlotte.

Later that night after sharing a roulade with Charlotte, I write in my diary: "I have glissandoed into a pit of melancholy," then add optimistically, "but I will pull myself up."

But I can't stop eating the burgers and roulades

and, of course, the more burgers and roulades I consume, the chubbier and more "lowdown" I feel. The lust I have felt for the Schumann, I now feel for the food. There is some devilish energy to it, some satisfying sense of resistance. And, ironically, some sense of control. Control of something. Finally. I know, somehow, but could not give voice to the knowing that *whatever else music is about, it is inevitably about the body.*

Both Charlotte and I feel we breathe charged air – air charged with rebellion and small violences. (The piano is, after all, a percussion instrument.) But because middle-class upbringing restrains us as tidily as hobbles on a milked cow, our acts of rebellion are never a danger to anyone. Except, sometimes, to ourselves.

Our most daring violation this summer is our walk down Pacific Avenue one afternoon dressed only in our crinoline petticoats and short boxer jackets. We didn't understand until many years later that this was not our greatest form of violation.

A few blocks away on Fillmore, meanwhile, ravings, declamations, and rebellion.

Ralph du Casse plays major chords with his forearms and declaims about art.

Jay de Feo slaps and molds plaster and paint onto the wall of her small apartment as she creates her 1,000-pound *Rose,* dozens of layers of oil, wood, and mica on canvas.

Three drunken poets interrupt an art exhibition by axing a piano to splinters and scoring its strings with a torch.

Artists and musicians and poets continue to speculate on Weldon Kees' presumed leap off the bridge, and strains of Allen Ginsberg's *Howl* still echo in the fog-blue streets.

Meanwhile, Charlotte and I only continue to indulge our extravagant hungers.

The Girl With the Flaxen Hair

orsefeathers!" Charlotte says. "Stop worrying about whether Christ is the Son of God. There's only the Unconscious. Anyway, come on. Let's walk over to the Institute. It's nearly time for the seminar. Maybe the Shadow will be lurking out front, sucking on his Chesterfield."

"The Shadow" is a reefer-thin young man with oily black hair and a carelessly attended beard. He dresses in black pants and a black tee. Although we regularly see him hanging around the Institute, we have never seen him near a musical instrument.

"Maybe he sings," I reply to Charlotte.

"Maybe," says Charlotte.

"Do you think he'll have on black again today? Everybody here wears black," I complain, thinking, too, of the boarder.

"Well, not Maureen," Charlotte says. "She'll probably be in that white tennis outfit with the short skirt."

I do not like thinking about Maureen, about Maureen's perfection, her slim body, her long flaxen hair, her expensive wardrobe and the way she can play the Beethoven concerto by practicing only two hours a day. "She's not human," I say.

"I know," says Charlotte, "does not sweat, does not bleed!"

After arriving at the Institute and exchanging hostile glances with the Shadow, who slouches against one of the exterior columns, a Chesterfield dangling from his lips, we go round to Anne's and Carolyn's practice rooms and the four of us go along into the Elfrida Steindorf room where the seminar sessions are held. A band of diffused light breaks through one of the large panels of window and is captured for an instant in the black upraised lid of the beautiful old Steinway. I think it looks like a kind of prayer. But then I have noticed before how the sight of a Steinway grand nearly always makes me feel religious.

Two minutes before 2:00 o'clock, Maureen breezes in, her face still moist from her recent match. I think it looks like dew and that it gives her beauty added freshness. Maureen wears a white tennis skirt and short-sleeve blouse and has a navy mohair sweater thrown over her shoulders. She nods to the class in general, and sits down to unpack her music, which she keeps before her on the piano when she plays.

But here is her great imperfection, her great flaw! I, more than the others, am horrified at this breach of professionalism. To fail to memorize the work at the outset is simply unheard of: a pianist who cannot perform from total memory, no matter how brilliant the playing and no matter on how little practice, is not a pianist worthy of serious consideration. Still ...

Thinking about it later, I feel not at all consoled by remembering Maureen's single flaw.

Requiem For Two Hands

I suppose by mid-summer Brico has forfeited all hope. The California experience has done nothing to inspire my work on the Schumann or on anything else musical. (And how can I remember now what happened so many years ago?) Logic dictates that the *Requiem* is chosen to give full voice to the level of vocal talent in her Opera workshop, not specifically in recognition of my defeat. To me, though, it is one more confirmation of my fatal destiny. It has begun with the Mozart concerto. It is to end, then, with the Mozart *Requiem.*

Brico is sure to have told me the story of how Mozart fell ill before finishing this darkly scored work. Of how it is recorded that he had begun to speak of death, saying that he was writing this requiem for himself. She is sure to have told me this. Certainly.

A theme of death colors the final workshop performances. On Monday, August 6, the *Cortège and Ballet from The Petite Suite* by Debussy, is "scored", the program reports, for two pianos, eight hands. Two of the hands playing are mine.

Cortège and Ballet!

The following Thursday, August 9, Mozart's *Requiem in D Minor*, "sung by the entire cast," the program reads, "Nancy Lou Deeds and Charlotte Wilson at the pianos."

But it doesn't end, finally, at least, with the *Requiem*. There are, after that, halting steps forward, dim renewals, vows, confused yearnings, inevitable failures. I grope blindly to find a way back, to feel ignited, to burn again with a blue flame.

Ashes, however, do not return to firewood.

Rhapsody in Blue

Today, over forty years later, I open the old photo book I have saved from the '50s. Several black and white photos, square ones with those crinkly edges, circa 1956, prove to me that we all left San Francisco and headed for Los Angeles.

Were it not for this evidence, I would write a different story, one eliminating everyone except Charlotte and myself. I would write that Anne and Carolyn had faded away, probably by train and were stepping out and onto Colorado soil before Charlotte and I had managed to make our way to the L.A. train station. I would also say that Brico had, at the end of the last performance, mysteriously disappeared in a poof. I would write how I felt ecstatic, and fearful, looking out myopically at this best of all possible worlds – a world of complete freedom and adventure – a world where anything might happen. This would be the beginning of my story were it not for the evidence.

At first I take the evidence to be the photos – those square ones with their deckled white edges. I take them up again. Brico sits in a chair, flanked on two sides by Anne and Carolyn. Anne looks exactly as she always did, perfectly bland; her brown cropped hair brushed up and away from her face in a style like the one worn by the Elsa Lancaster in the classic Frankenstein film. Carolyn wears her self-conscious, slightly silly grin – the one that accentuates the dimple in her forthright chin. Charlotte, who stands behind Brico's chair, seems oblivious; absent even, planes, dimensions apart from this scene.

But the grayness of the scene disconcerts me. What I first take to be a factor of the old black and white film, I suddenly realize is actually the image of climate. It is foggy and cold, too, evidently, for now I notice that everyone is wearing a woolen wrap. There is Brico in her long green Loden coat which she wears with her white lace-up and tongue brogues. Anne, neat in her short tweed jacket. Carolyn in her bulky topper coat and Charlotte looking like a washerwoman in her plain three-quarter length gabardine, her head covered with an old silk scarf that she has tied under her chin. The group looks to me now like a sad family of refugees. I was the same.

What are we doing in L.A. in the middle of summer dressed for winter in Colorado? Eventually the indisputable conclusion: we are, in fact, in Carmel. In August. Then I remember the fog, the cold; the hanging fuchsias, the bowers of white wisteria, and stands of purple clematis that wall in Ms. Lyle's garden, that secret place behind her music shop on Ocean Avenue. The exotic Ms. Lyle, with her two white Afghan hounds and her cottage in Carmel Valley where we all spend one night.

Would I remember any of this if I hadn't come across a photo of her shot, apparently, on the same roll, which shows her kneeling, costumed in an Asian kimono I remember as bright red? Like the one Aunt Kay used to wear when, as a child, I ran away to her house and we played dress up and drank warm milk out of her gold-rimmed China tea cups. In the photo, Ms. Lyle's black hair is drawn back in a bun and she is kneeling in front of her fireplace. A posed and dramatic profile. Who was she really? A lover? A friend? A patron? Always, there is one more mystery too distant and too tangled to unravel.

I set these photos aside. They are not the ones. I remember distinctly a snapshot taken in Los Angeles that summer. I remember, because in the photo Brico is wearing a short-sleeved white blouse and a gathered skirt with a gay South-of-the-Border braid trim around the hem. The only time I remember ever seeing her dressed in this way, without the sturdy straight skirt, the thick silk blouse, the suede jacket. Or summer at recitals, in the jersey short-sleeved dresses with a brooch, a cameo of Beethoven, pinned lopsidedly at the neck. (The lopsidedness worried Mother). And there, too, as in the photo I am searching for now, the same white lace-up-and-tongue brogues. And so I continue my search for the other photo, the scrap of evidence that will once and for all give me the factual information I need to go on with my story.

When I finally locate the photo, it, too, is of no help. There are, in fact, two photos snapped a few minutes apart and surely in L.A. Brico is dressed in the white blouse and gay, gathered skirt as I remember, but she is with Sabina, a young violinist from Germany. First, they are sitting together on a wooden bench, perhaps a bus stop, and next, they stride energetically down the street. Carolyn and Anne and Charlotte are nowhere to be seen.

I am invisible, a ghost with a Brownie camera.

The photos have been no help at all, only adding more parts of muddle to the whole. I pull out my diary, thinking I should have thought of that first. But that, too, is of no use. It ends abruptly in June of 1956 and doesn't pick up again until September. A rupture, I remember now, by the betrayal of a high school sweetheart. I remember, but can no longer feel the body-blow pain and feelings of humiliation I felt at the time.

I put the useless diary back on the shelf. As a last resort, I pull down the leather-bound autograph book with its inscribed gold insignia on the front cover, the book that had accompanied me on both summer trips to California with Brico. I turn to the second half of the book where signatures are sparser than in the first half. Here, too, the visible waning of interest.

Still, many have written and signed their names, a few have put down a date. I remember so many bits of this person, some of that one, of another one nothing at all. So many scratchy signatures in a little book. Some famous in their way. Few of these.

It is all just making everything worse. I find signatures with dates of 1956 that I remember as having been scribbled in 1954. Confusions, wild imaginings, misattributions, evidently.

Patently the story I want to tell has more to do with healing astroblemes on the heart than adhering to any hard facts of reality.

"What are the facts of this case?" the detective wants to know.
"Blindness and mystery," is the reply.

And so I cut again to Charlotte. Charlotte is, anyway, one of the facts of that summer. Charlotte, with her North Carolina accent, her lost ballerina's hope, her head on fire. How dazzling, this overripe goddess, this conjurer of the marvelous.

It is that summer, our last day in L.A., that I remember vividly. How, inexplicably, we miss our train home; how my panic escalates at our predicament. We are alone in a large city full of strangers, we have almost no money, and there is hunger and, worse, a long dangerous night between us and the next train heading east.

But to tell the facts of the story, is not enough, of course. Still, it seems important to set them down here.

Leaving the L.A. train depot, then, I stand in a state of confusion and fear. Charlotte, however, like Brico, a woman in full command in any situation, steers me out of the station and into a Yellow Cab that sits waiting at the curb. The driver, however dubious he seems about whether he will receive his fare, loads our bags and our boxes and then us into his vehicle.

"The Biltmore Hotel," Charlotte commands him.

Before I could form a question to match the surprise on my face, she gouges me in the ribs with her elbow, fixing me, at the same time, with one of Brico's infamous gazes. I close my mouth and sit silent.

When at last we unload ourselves and our baggage from the cab, Charlotte strides towards the hotel entrance calling over her shoulder, "Follow me."

Once inside, she plants me between a giant Ionic column and one of the Biltmore's heroic palms, boxes and bags beside me; then she sails like a yacht across the plumy peach of carpeted lobby and out of view. After what feels like an hour but which is perhaps fifteen minutes, she returns, picks up her bag and two boxes and says again, "Follow me."

We must present a ludicrous and curious sight, two bedraggled, overweight and unfashionable young women lugging our bags and boxes through the historic Los Angeles Biltmore; trampling on its tradition and elegance. I feel that at any moment we will be apprehended and thrown into the street where we will become what we truly are at this moment - homeless.

Down a long hallway, we come at last to a door at which Charlotte stops, produces a key from the pocket of her coat and unlocks. I stagger through, dazed and wondering.

The room is heady with patterns everywhere of blooms and large green leaves, of opulence that blossoms and seems, even, to breathe. It is, too, a sanctuary, holding in safety our bags, or boxes, my anxieties, and my questions.

*B*ut what are the things I am forgetting? That my head swims with questions for Charlotte, all beginning with "how."

That Charlotte refuses ever to explain anything, sucking the plum of her secret

into the corner of one dark cheek.

That I cannot find a rational explanation for what occurred.

That I wonder if she might have exchanged portions of her maternal body for our room,

that I think, *How ridiculous!*

That I think that she must have called a rich relative in North Carolina for help.

That a rich relative owns the hotel.

That I felt grateful I have been saved from An American Tragedy.

That the room has a window that opened.

That the smell I will remember forever is not of the rose garden outside the window, or the expensive bar of soap on the marble washstand.

That the city exudes a sense of urgency.

How that mix of urgency and pavement heat and the exhaust of vehicles, that rising industrial miasma, is as memorable as anything else that happens that day.

How it still intoxicates me.

And later,

How we make it onboard our train the next morning.

How happy I am to be home.

How Charlotte completely disappears then.

How, forty years later, I long to find her.

How I wish I had hugged her.

How I will not forgot anything I know about Charlotte herself. She burns like a flame in memory. Her mystery and magic. How she lives on as rhapsody, a strobe of sky in ultramarinist blue.

Antonia Brico

Nancy at Acrosonic, Denver, 1954

Businessmen-Musicians Open 6th Season Nov. 5

The Denver Businessmen's orchestra, sixty-five musicians who play for the pleasure of making music, will start its sixth season Nov. 5 in Phipps auditorium.

John T. Roberts, director of music for the Denver public schools, will be guest conductor for the opening concert.

Dr. Antonia Brico, regular conductor of this organization of talented amateur instrumentalists and professionals with careers in other and widely varied fields, will return to the podium for the second the four concerts.

Soloist for the opening concert will be the Rev. Q. Balfour Patterson, Episcopal chaplain at the University of Colorado. His bass-baritone voice will be heard in the "Confutatis Maledictus" aria from Verdi's "Requiem" and the Mefisto aria, "The Golden Calf," from Gounod's "Faust."

Major orchestral music will be the familiar Caesar Franck symphony in D minor, and a first Denver performance of Max Steiner's "Symphonie Moderne," music from his score for the motion picture "The Four Wives." Rounding out the program will be a Bach prelude, chorale and fugue and the Strauss overture to "Die Fledermaus."

Dates and soloists for the other concerts of the Denver Businessmen's 1953-54 season are: Jan. 14 — Ruthabeth Conrad, concertmaster of the Albuquerque Symphony orchestra; March 11 — Nancy Lee Deeds, 14-year-old piano soloist playing the Mozart piano concerto in A major; April 29 — Beethoven opera, "Fidelio," given in concert performance.

Concert Features Young Solo Pianist

By ALLEN YOUNG
Denver Post Staff Writer

The frequency with which cold weather coincides with concerts the Denver Businessmen's chestra at Phipps Auditorium become more and more eaningless because of the sinrity and sense of accomplishent their concerts regularly tablish.

On Thursday evening the conrt drew a large attendance, any of whom were drawn by e performance of a Mozart ano concerto by a 14-year-old, ancy Lou Deeds, and others atacted by the proficiency the chestra displays in its performces of music less often heard concert.

Dr. Antonia Brico inspired he orchestra with especially nusical influences for Thursday vening's concert. We doubt hat we have heard the orchesra sound better, heard it play with more musicality or sensibility.

Under Dr. Brico's direction the yle of the individual composions was carefully established. e balance of instruments leased the ear and the response the orchestra to her wishes iade for high-level musical leasure.

To coin an old phrase, Miss eeds went to town with the Mozart. She played admirably, clean- and sympathetically, showing race in runs and projecting a ice feeling for the beauties of e Mozart concerto in A major, 488, the concerto of the eveing.

The assurance in her playing which enhanced the performance was no false or immodest one, nor was her playing based on any assumptions that would lead her astray. It was direct,

Greater strength would have given her more assurance in the final measures, and also another quality which may come with experience and age, the ability to tie together the widely separated notes of an andante.

The Mozartean feeling of the accompaniment was exceptionally pleasing, nicely balanced as far as the orchestration went, properly phrased.

As an opening the overture t Gluck's "Iphigenia in Aulis" showed markedly good string playing and brought a fine piece of music to attention.

Of special interest on the program was the inclusion of a "Tone Poem" by Gregory Bueche, director of the department of music of Colorado A. & M. College. It is a well considered piece of music, serious in intent, offering pleasingly sonorous material for an orchestra.

The music was contemporary in style, suggesting Roy Harris at times, yet basically was a very conservative work with few dissonances held over an instant, and it found the positive mood very much to its liking.

A vigorous, sweeping performance of Sibelius' "En Saga" was notable as being the performance of a piece which contains some of the most exciting music Sibelius has written. A quieter central section had nice woodwind playing but the tempo seemed to lag a bit here, although a stirring climax was reached.

Antonia Brico conducting

Nancy Lou Deeds, 14-Year-Old Pianist, to Make Concert Stage Debut on March 11

* * *   * * * * * * *

An attractive, 14-year-old Washington county girl, who has been playing piano since she was eight years old, will make her debut on the concert stage in Denver March 11 with the Denver Businessmen's Orchestra.

Between now and then, Nancy Lou Deeds, daughter of Mr. and Mrs. A. E. Deeds, will be busy with radio and television appearances at a number of stations in Colorado.

Nancy Lou appeared Jan. 29 on the Eddy Rogers TV show, and her next appearance will be Wednesday, March 3, on the Ray Perkins show in Denver. This program will be videoed at 7:30 p.m. over channel 2.

At 8:15 a.m. March 4, she will take part in Dale Morgan's program over radio station KFEL. On the same day, she will appear as a guest of Jane Sterling on KOA's "These Kids of Ours" program. This show is telecast over the Pueblo and Colorado Springs stations at 4:30 p.m., over KOA-TV at 5 and broadcast over KOA radio at 7:30 p.m.

KLZ-TV will feature her at 1 p.m. March 5 in the program, "At Home with Judy Knowles."

A student of Dr. Antonia Brico of Denver, Nancy Lou makes the trip to Denver every two weeks from her home 10 miles southeast of Atwood. She is a student at the Washington County High School in Akron. Her brother Eddie, 9, and sister Teresa, 8, ride into Akron with her each day on the school bus.

For her debut March 11, she will present Mozart's "Piano Concerto in A Major." She will be the youngest of the soloists to appear this season, others being Rev. A. B. Patterson of Boulder, a bass soloist, and Ruthabeth Conrad of Albuquerque, violinist.

NANCY LOU DEEDS
—Journal-Advocate Photo

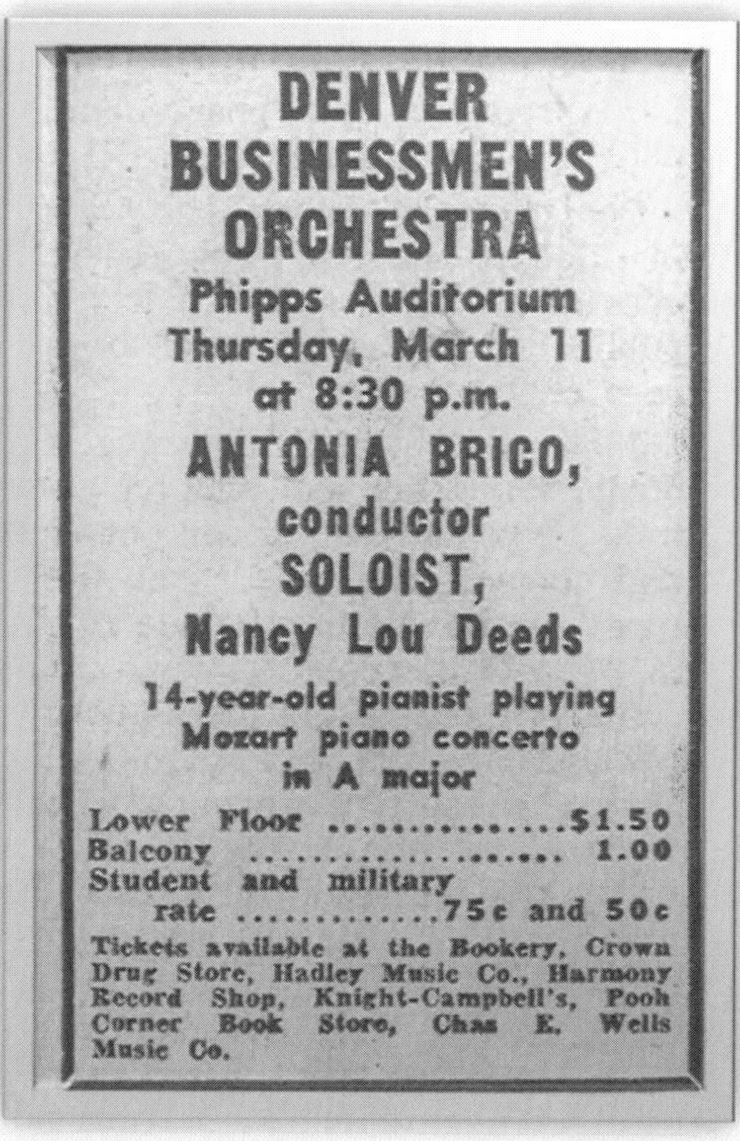

Denver Post Concert Ad

CONCERT 24

PHIPPS AUDITORIUM 8:30 P. M. MARCH 11, 195_

NANCY LOU DEEDS, PLAYING

MOZART PIANO CONCERTO N_

DENVER BUSINESSMEN'S ORCHESTRA

ANTONIA BRICO, CONDUCTOR

Concerto in A major
for Piano and Orchestra
[K. 488]

Edited and orchestra score arranged for Piano II by
Francis L. York

Wolfgang Amadeus Mozart

I

Nancy and her parents, 1940

Graveside Memorial

Through a Dark Wood

II

Contrapuntus

The light is heavy this afternoon, streaming in through the windows at odd angles. B sits in a chair beside the spinet bench on which Carolyn works at her Grieg, her heavy shoulders hunched and heaving a little, as they always do when she plays. Carolyn, dogged, and one of the still industrious ones, I think.

My body feels leaden with resistance and a stubbornness that defend me against B's hectoring, her manipulations, the great gravitas of her presence. It is March 1957, and B has traveled by train from her home in Denver to Springfield where she had come looking for fresh talent nearly a decade before, and where she "discovered" me.

I have come for a lesson I do not want and for which I am not prepared; a situation that is becoming all too familiar. Carolyn continues to play, the melody seeming to me exaggerated, too heavy, like the light and, too, like the empty, awful weight of my body. Like B's Will.

B pierces through it all instantly, gazing at me in

that way she has, stripping me of any pretenses I try to muster. And it must have been at that moment, her eyes fixing me, one beautiful hand resting on the arm of the spinet, the other hovering above Carolyn's left arm like a bird preparing for flight – it is just then that B decides to play her last card, to risk the irrevocable act that I feel as betrayal, a dark gift I feed and carry inside for the rest of my life.

Carolyn stops playing and sits as though frozen in place, her muscular hands waiting, resting temporarily on the keys before sliding down into her lap. The shoulders drop an appreciable degree and she keeps her eyes staring straight ahead, safe. She, a thing apart.

*B*ut it all begins to seem too melodramatic when I know that there is worse to come. How to continue in unsentimental prose what feels so irredeemably and intensely sentimental to the narrator?

Here, the narrative breaks, ruptures. There is the sense of the too-brilliant flash of a bulb, blinding, and the resulting snapshot that shows only shapes – two forces, each with samsaric intentions, one in conflict and pain. The darker form with the red diamond in the center is the Master, her will to power and to success. The still dark but smaller form, rimmed in blue appearing on the right near the door is me, the recently reluctant disciple, with my despair and my desperate desire to be free.

What the snapshot cannot reveal is the element of

betrayal carried away by the blue-rimmed form. It cannot record B's early promise to me that no other student would be entered in the Central City piano competition at the end of summer; that *I* am to be the only of B's students to be so honored, so "loved." It cannot show my desperate need for this.

But today, also not visible in the snapshot, B has, in the presence of Carolyn, announced that Carolyn, too, will be so honored. Carolyn who, B says a little maliciously, I think, "has been practicing very diligently on the Grieg."

Carolyn!

Perhaps B hopes through enraging me, to inspire me to harder labors, but it feels like an insult, a slap, and the inspiration B seeks to infuse in me works instead to harden my resistance to a thing now much larger than a mere competition.

Malediction

A counterpoint of paradigms: The master's destruction of his pupil. The disciple's betrayal... what master, after all, can respect the freedom of decision in a disciple?"
~ George Steiner

After forty years, the closeness of the event still dazzles and stalls me. The vision splinters. A chorus, a church, a cry from the pews. A small violence.

I don't remember the Baca County Chorus singers who were at rehearsal that day in the church.

I don't remember that they worked on Joyce Barthelson's "The Miners."

I don't remember that Joyce Barthelson flew in from New York for the performance the following month; I do remember that B and Barthelson were friends.

I don't remember singing in the chorus; not a single note or verse of the composition.

I also don't remember what time of year it was.

Not summer when B cashes in her quarters and brazens or wheedles her way into the lives of the great and famous of Europe or Africa or Finland; into the personal lives of Schweitzer or Sibelius or the heirs of Richard Wagner.

I don't remember which church it was. Presbyterian, I think, or Methodist. Not Catholic.

And I don't remember what I was wearing, which seems odd, since so many memorable events in my life are connected to clothes. Like the black velvet and taffeta dress I wore to Grandmother's funeral; the pink cropped jacket that summer in San Francisco in 1956; or the pair of red strap, wedge-heeled shoes that I wore on my first train trip to Denver with B for lessons.

The memory slips, blurs, selects.

I feel, more than remember, B sitting beside me on a pew at the back of the church. B feels like something immense and potent, full of magic and secrets, like the Sphinx. Some fabulous beast ... pressing against me ... to mold me.

What is B saying, in a voice thick with regret? Repeating her disappointment at my refusal to compete. In the Central City competition? Yes. And, again, how two of her other students won prizes? Yes. And, again, B. in tones deepening into sadness, "And you, dear one, would have had the gold!"

I sit slumped, weighted, saturated with B's disappointments. My head aches and I can't think. I feel I am in the presence of a stranger, possibly a dangerous one. I feel someone has tied a scarf around my neck and is pulling it tighter and tighter. It makes my breathing shallow.

The fear and entrapment I feel is suddenly replaced by a kind of wild kamikaze bravado. "I want to quit," I blurt out in tones more subdued than the ones I had intended. B stares. I'm sure that she has felt this coming. She has forestalled it several times before by coaxing, touching, by wheeling out her dessert cart of rainbow visions of the sweet and brilliant future we will share.

But, B must think, I have tried it all before. This time is different. The child has moved away, has turned her back on her God-given talent, on the love and attention I have showered on her, on the years of promise, of our future together, hand in hand.

And I feel a kind of fury growing from all of these ideas – the lost years, the lost future. And that B wants to roar, to devastate what she can no longer control.

She turns to me and speaks softly, but her voice vibrates with her great and swelling rage.

"It would serve you right," she says, each word dropping on me like a detonation, "if God took away both of your hands. It would serve you right for turning your back on the talent He gave you, on everything *I* have given you!"

I don't hear more of B's fierce and massive wrath, for out of my own fury and hurt, I begin to silently weep, as I have done at other severe times in the past. This time, though, there is no hope of repentance and so no possibility of reconciliation.

Spontaneous Outburst
of Freedom

Interlochen 1957

DEPARTURE

I pack my bags with essentials suggested in the camp's brochure: white shirt, raincoat, flashlight, campus coat, anklets, overshoes, stamps, and watch (navy corduroy knickers supplied by the camp). The day I board the Continental Trailways bus headed east out of Lamar, I dress in sturdy gold pedal pushers and a purple v-necked over-blouse that my mother has designed and made especially for this occasion. The rickrack stripes down the outside of each pant leg, and the dark long lines of the over-blouse, are meant to give a slimming effect to my adolescent body, which has become distressingly pudgy. This pudginess is a matter of dismay for both me and my mother.

ARRIVAL

A lake-green jeep wagon with "Interlochen" printed in white on each side pulls into the drive at the bus depot in Traverse City,

Michigan, where I wait. The camp staff member and shuttle driver wears a white shirt and long blue corduroy trousers. He is tall and thin, with angular features, short black hair and heavy brooding brows. He is friendly and attractive. He says his name is "Hans," which I recognize as German, but am surprised that he is not fair-haired and muscular with a thick accent.

The sight of me, rumpled and dusty, and looking numb with fatigue and bewilderment, must have touched Hans, for he soon sweeps me and my large teal Samsonite case into the jeep, chatting cheerfully as he speeds back to the camp. He deposits me at Cabin W-4, the lodge for University Division students, carries in my bag, and promises to return later to show me around.

I squint myopically and survey the large room with its row of double bunk beds. Locating mine, I shove my suitcase underneath and for a time stand silent, steeped in a brew of exhaustion, expectation ... and fantastic romantic ambitions.

Years later, remembering Hans, I imagine him telling a friend, "I picked up another, what they love to call here, "protégée" in Traverse City yesterday. The camp is teeming with them! This one, from some remote off-the-map place, west of the Mississippi. Of all of them I have shuttled in so far, this one is by far the most naïve. Mein Gott! She was rhapsodizing over smoke roiling out of the old canning plant on the way out of town, thinking it was fog! But she's a sweet kid and kind of lost. Maybe I'll take her to ride along with me on a few shuttle trips to pick up the rest of them. The trips are becoming pretty tedious and some company would be nice."

June 19, 1957

Dearest Mother and Daddy,

I didn't think I would ever get here, but finally I made it! I wish you could see this place! There are trees everywhere and little wood cabins, like at Poudre when we go fishing only these are smaller, and there is a Steinway grand in every single cabin. There are also rows of stone rooms without doors! And there is a Steinway upright in every one of these. I have never seen so many Steinway pianos since I went to the Wells warehouse with Louie to choose a piano for my concert at Phipps.

There's a really big lake here that goes to the horizon and makes me think it's an ocean. Last night at the lake there was the most wonderful light show in the sky. It's called aurora borealis or northern lights and nobody seems to know what causes it. It was like a magic show. I wish you could have seen it.

I'm in a big cabin with lots of girls – the large room is filled with a row of bunk beds on both sides! I met a nice girl named Choyce who is also working with me in food service. She's really nice. You should see us in our navy knickers and knee sox. They look really funny on, but are pretty comfortable and warm. Everybody has to wear them. I'll send you a picture when I can.

I signed up for oboe and modern dance lessons (the teacher is a dancer from New York! named Joe Gifford). I'm going to sing in the camp chorus, too. They do two or three operettas and some other things that I don't know about yet. There is a camp orchestra and you can hear music all over the camp all day long.

The camp puts out a newsletter they call "Scherzo." They handed out applications yesterday and I filled one out for the editor's job. I don't know why and I'm sure I won't get it. There are lots of kids here and most of them from big schools. I put down that I was the editor of our school annual last year. I'll let you know what happens.

Better close now so that I can get this letter in the mail.

I'm kind of homesick. I sure miss you both and Teresa and Eddy. Give them a hug for me. I'll write you again tomorrow.

All my love,

Nancy Lou

Alive With Romantic Ambitions...

The romantic ambitions that so completely overshadowed my musical ones, did not progress exactly as I had hoped. After a few trips into town with Hans and a couple of meetings after dark behind one of the practice cabins, Hans removes himself from my life. I see him with other, older and (I couldn't help noticing) slimmer young women, and while he is always friendly when we meet, he does not seek me out, does not invite me again to meet him after dark.

My summer is given over to fantasies of capturing him, and even unto Christmas, months after the end of camp, I send him a Christmas card. Forty years later, coming across the card, signed simply, "Hans" that he has been kind enough to send in response, I wonder how I ever managed to get his home address. For the rest of my life I will remember him saying on our last secret rendezvous behind a practice cabin, "You're a doll – and you know what dolls are for, don't you?"

It doesn't seem like much of a line for ending a relationship.

Through A Dark Wood

To defray camp fees, Brico has committed me to work Food Service for six and a half hours each day. Every morning before the sun makes its way above the horizon, I make my way through a dark wood, running like a wild Fauve through the trees. The world seems suddenly simple and life possible.

Beyond Brico's stentorian dictates and her long, pointy baton; beyond the all-seeing eyes of my mother and her loving efforts at policing food; beyond the loving, protective arms of my father and his strict rules on dating, I break free. For one glorious summer!

Reveling in the intoxicating grasp of this freedom, I fail to consider how to carry it forward into my life. I am anyway unconscious of the substratum of guilt it immediately builds on; cannot imagine how years into the future my choices will be made in the cause of this freedom. But, because rash and ill-considered, will only lead me into a different kind of bondage. There will be jobs and marriages and children.

Catalog of Failures and An Unconscious Change of Direction

I do not want to do what I have been doing for you ...

At camp, my struggle with B's plans for me is played out in a public arena. There is a protégé on every bunk and I feel insignificant and marginal. My *modus operandi* in this situation is one of complete withdrawal from the competition.

There are various levels of musicians there, of course, but at the time I don't recognize this. Under the achievers, there are the sybarites, the romance-seekers, others who do the ordinary work while the mind roams, scan other opportunities. Below all of these, I sit and move, feeling a dismal failure, but dissembling it all with a mask of mock participation and a social inclusion I do not feel. I can see that I need to cross over, accept a change of direction, but I feel caught in a temporal storm that feels powerful and dangerous and it paralyzes me.

I don't practice. I drop oboe. I take no responsibility for anything except showing up for food service duty three times a day. I don't manage any kind of real romance, and I snitch some of a cabin mate's tiny homemade cookies her mother sends her in a Quaker Oatmeal box. (A greedy act that I will always feel guilt over.) Amazing that I am never identified as the culprit. The matter might be automatically settled were I the only young woman in W-4 with an expanding body that summer, but regular trips into Traverse City for whole pizzas are routine evening entertainments for many of us housed in Cabin W-4. For most of us, the evidence manifests proportionately in our bodies.

I think that it is a lark, that I am having great fun. I think now, it was, for me, a kind of desperation that I felt – spinning myopically in my tourbillion of failure.

Failures:
of piano practice
of oboe lessons
of modern dance
of romance
of integrity
of faith
Or, I suppose it can also be seen as:
Self against Brico
Self against Mother
Self against Dad
but mostly,
Self against Self.

Back Home

The return to reality brings with it a sharp sense of disappointment. The summer has been a dream, the break to freedom an illusion, but has also only increased the steady *obbligato* of guilt that plays through my head. Back home, faced with my situation, I rapidly slide into a melancholic binge. I live in a blue fog, battening on sweets and rich pastries trying to bury alive my secret feelings of shame and failure. For the summer's failure is all that I see.

It is a disorder, a cry for help in a time and a place that cannot recognize it for what it is. I gain weight, wearing my pathology like a billboard, like a confession – like some innate atavistic attempt, through my bodily humiliations, to be shriven. Inundated early on with Puritan ethics and protestant theology, it is the most likely course.

There is nothing to corroborate these stories. In her diary for the summer of 1957, there is only silence. But a story is told as much by silence as by speech.
~ Susan Griffin, *Chorus of Stones*

I have two weeks before packing again, this time to depart for my first semester at the University of Colorado and piano lessons with Storm Bull, Brico's despised (and successful) rival. In spite of a string of A level grades in all of my courses, on Homecoming Day, with no date for the game or the dance and no large bouquet of giant yellow mums in my hand, I board the bus for Denver and leave the campus.

Confused thinking and despair, too, drive me to the idea of returning to Brico and my former life. But, of course, this illusion can only hold form for a few short weeks. Through efforts of my patient parents, and possibly Brico, I am enrolled at CU the subsequent semester, this time not as music major. This, too fails. I sleep in late, skip classes, and spend my father's money on gorgeous wool plaid skirts two sizes too small, fostering some new illusion that will be my future.

After CU, a similar failure at Colorado College in Colorado Springs.

Everything has been tried. Everything has failed to lift me up and back into life. Eventually I solve the problem by marrying a childhood sweetheart. It is not a lasting solution, but not a bad one either. Out of this union emerge two beautiful daughters. Perhaps then, I feel that I have at last *created* something of lasting value, something of my own. But mostly, there is a great gift given, the lifelong joy of these two beautiful and loving human beings in my life.

Asleep In The World

Like that adolescent year in Boulder, possibilities given up, all lost;
Even options of grief or rage, gone underground;
Buried by a fattening on sweets and rice puddings;
Buried under the search for a magical object to transform the roly-poly caterpillar into an iridescent butterfly.
The cashmere sweater; the Scottish woolen skirt, Rich, jewel-blue plaid, but sizes too small. From Hope.
A prisoner of shadow now. Darkest umbra.
Heart-sick.
One quarter of all deaths in China are due to pulmonary disease.

In general, there are no happy endings.
Still, small vibrations from time to time lead me to suspect a concealed dark vibrancy – the face is bearded and wild.
She knows the truth about B.
But everyone in the next room is dead.

Investigations: A Search for Meaning

Scene of the Crime

See. There on the left-hand page, a child. I stand, squinting into the sun, my soft curls held back to the left of my part with a plain red barrette. I wear a short jacket, a pleated wool skirt, anklets, and my favorite red-strapped wedges; shoes I will remember with pleasure all of my life.

Beside me, B, my teacher, a protective and possessive wing thrown over my shoulder. (Later it will be remembered as a hug.) The teacher, a conductor, linguist, world traveler, is an anomaly. A woman. She wears a belted suede jacket, her right hand slid into the jacket pocket, straight woolen skirt, thickish hose, and black lace-up brogues, dark and heavy. (They will leave footprints on many lives.) The teacher holds herself erect, could almost be taken for a gentleman landowner, a woodsman. But is not.

Turn a few pages and you will see me, now a young adult. I sit, in profile, at a piano, my hands on the keys, "hand position" perfect, the result of hundreds of hours of practice, of lessons. I wear a simple white dress, perhaps my eighth-grade graduation dress, and

I stare into space as though in full concentration on the Mozart. Or perhaps it is the Bürgmuller. Every note, every phrasing edge-sharp in my memory. The shadow of the teacher is not captured in this photograph.

But then, only a couple of pages later, there I am again. But this surely cannot be the same fourteen-year-old young woman of only a few pages back! In this shot, I sit again at a piano, a different one, but now I wear a strapless gown, all satin and netting, a gown I hated and remember as scratchy and in shades of mauve. Everything in the photo is unharmonious, discordant. There is a beefiness about me. My hair is short and my nose seems larger, out of place on my face. It doesn't look like anyone I have ever known.

The photo is dark with shadowed edges. This photo, the last of its kind, speaks of a major transition, a passage of import, an initiation perhaps. A disillusionment. Surely.

The detective asks: where is the scene of the crime?

Then, in true Agatha Christie fashion: tell me more about the victim.

A thimbleful of words reduced to the head of a pin.

Interrogation

The detective questions: What crimes do you lodge against her?
A voice answers: Crimes of the body.
Another cries out: Of the spirit!
They chorus: Of the heart!

Elucidate, demands the detective. Give me hard facts.
A voice complains: She dragged me out of a hospital bed to perform.
The detective considers: You performed? You did not die?

So, then. There must be more!

Silence.

Blame the victim? they ask.

Tell me more about the victim, he demands.
They are unwilling.
Finally. They chorus: There is no more.

The Desire House

When I find Anne, the oracle, she is sitting in a stupa-like cabin in the Sierra foothills among vegans and Yogananda acolytes. An aura of serenity circumscribes her and a halo of light seems to vibrate from her beautiful, large head.

She holds in her hand, the mysterious Vedic charts mapping both B's life and my own.

I came, I tell her, looking for the connection. For the "why" of my experiences with B, *why* did I leave, what meaning, place, should it hold in my life? A large experience, inappropriately assimilated. Perhaps.

Perhaps there will be no certainties, even here ...

Because B's exact time of birth remains unknown, only some of the attributes of her chart can be read with anything approaching accuracy.

"She would have had to have a fiery ascendant," Anne says, *"either Sagittarius or Leo, I think."*

Eliminating attributes possible, Anne settles on Leo as B's ascendant sign. *"Even in her physical attributes,"* Anne says, looking at the 8x10 photograph of B I have sent her, *"it looks like she has a mane, has the physical appearance of a lioness."*

Studying the chart she holds in her hand, Anne continues, "Her moon is in the 7th House, an Aquarian moon. Also, her Jupiter is on your moon and your Jupiter is on her moon. This is very unusual and would mean a kind of connection you would always feel for each other. Although your fundamental natures are dramatically different, whenever you put Jupiter on the moon, you always feel a deep friendship and willingness to share. Very unusual.

"The esoteric knowledge about her Aquarian moon is interesting," Anne says, "and the thing that pops out for me most of all, is her moon in this area of Aquarius, which would mean coming to a karmic crossroads and changing some difficult habit pattern or obsession. This is very powerful and is ruled by the Lord of the Cosmic Ocean. It is connected with the water of wisdom and it teaches us to learn to master the serpent force under divine grace or get destroyed by it. Anyone with this moon has an extreme life. You see addicts, in particular, with this specific moon. I feel, in her case, that she was probably a love addict."

Still studying B's chart that lay on the table before her, Anne continues. "But what is also interesting is that she has her Mercury and Venus and Mars all in Taurus and Gemini, which is very sensuous and personal ... the desire house. Perhaps," Anne concludes, "her reason for incarnating was to become disillusioned with the world and to work out some of these desires of a more personal nature."

Anne goes on, drawing other invisible lines connecting B and her relationship with Yogananda, between B's chart and my own: our nodes, our moons, our twelve houses. My brain, although fuzzed with mysterious Vedic riddles, clings to the one question for which answer I have really come.

"Is there," I ask, thinking to keep the question on general terms, "anything in B's chart to indicate that she might have sexually abused her young musical charges?"

With hardly a hesitation, Anne replies. "If Antonia were a disciple of Yogananda's, it would have been highly unlikely, as they take a vow of chastity. Highly unlikely," she repeats, looking at me.

Sex and the Singular Swami

THE SAN FRANCISCO WEEKLY

March 10, 1999

Last year, a Redwood City jury handed down a million-plus-dollar judgment against longtime spiritual director, Donald J. Walters (known generally as Swami Kriyananda), another senior official of the church, and the church itself, for the sexual exploitation of a former church member. In that case, six women testified under oath that the swami had taken sexual advantage of them when they were impressionable twentysomethings in search of spiritual advancement.

Helen Goa

I begin to weary of the whole tired conjecture. There are no visible connecting lines, no absolutes, no evidence, and it occurs to me, not for the first time, that my search has been fueled by a need to justify my desertion of B and the future we might have had together. What guilt underlies this search – guilt over betraying B, my parents and supporters, the beautiful, luminous dream?

Penetralia

The Last Protégée

Stalled, midway, on the verge of giving up, a dream.

It is B's funeral. Three of us sit around a long table, a conservative, middle-aged socialite, an older man of medium height in a suit, and me. The man is pocked and red-faced, dissipated and wasted, and is most certainly gay.

The minister officiating asks if anyone would like to say a few words. No one speaks.

"Someone should say something," *he says, presumably out of respect,* "a eulogy."

The gay man relieves the situation and stands. He speaks briefly, generically. His words are forgettable.

Later we stand around the burial site. The man turns to me, questioning why I did not speak up at B's funeral. "You do not speak because you are too full of emotion," he tells me. "I understand, but it is up to you. You must say something. You are the last protégée."

The vividness of the scene, the pock-faced man's imperative, doesn't leave me; I feel, no alternative but to continue on to the end.

But as I write, I begin to think about the meaning

of "protégé." Protégés – those talented and purposeful enough to deserve the title; those talented but short-termed hopefuls, and those puppeted into the role through the teeming desire of a master. Of the hundreds of thousands of protégés, so-called, over even a single decade, in a single field, the number who move on through years of practice and struggle to the glory of original promise can surely be counted on two hands.

I write this then, I think, not to rationalize my own failure, but to provide a context for it.

PROTÉGÉ (PROTÉGÉE - FEMININE FORM):

One who is protected or trained or whose career is furthered by a person of experience, prominence, or influence.
(Merriam Webster's Collegiate Dictionary, Tenth Ed.)

One who is under the protection or care of another, especially a person of superior position or influence.
(OED, Twenty-Fourth Printing in U.S., February 1985)

One who is protected and aided by the patronage of another person (C19: from French *protéger,* to PROTECT)
(Collins Concise English Dictionary Eighth Edition 2012)

Certainly hundreds of thousands. Probably more. Undoubtedly more.

"In Latin, in the beginning, in certain cultures, a crippled newborn. An infant impaired and broken, but at the same time in the primary state of the newborn, which is holy. A 'special' but doomed child whose immediate future, as a damaged infant, was death."
(Theodore Thass-Thienemann's discussion of "The Holy"
in *The Interpretation of Language*, Vol II: Understanding
the Unconscious Meaning of Language.)

Protected, blessed, and *singularly* special, I feel all of

these for the eight years I labor and spring, nearly whole from B's thigh. I assume this state of "specialness" and, in hindsight, grew possessed of an exaggerated sense of self-importance and superiority. While at the same time, a suspicion gradually forms that the demand for special status only veils frightening feelings of inferiority of both talent and intellect. Gifted and crippled. Blessed and cursed.

Why now, so many years after walking away from the Schumann, from the Franck, from the Steinway, and from B, after so many years, and with memories morphed or fugitive, am I compelled to write our story?

Compelled by my dreams, I could say.

A decade before setting out with the intention of writing any kind of formal account of my years with B, I am visited by several "retailing" dreams.

The first of these occur in 1981, "From B's House to Hardware Job". When, by 1985, I have not taken up my pen, the dreams become more demanding. "B Hounds Me To Accept Job in Retailing."

Two years later, when still I remained uncommitted to the task in waking life, the writing work begins in a dream, "I am Virginia Woolf Working for B" and, in 1989, the dream instructor gives me a "retailing" assignment. It is not until nearly five years later, fourteen years after the first retailing dream that I am inspired by a dream, on St. Lucy's eve, 1995, to begin.

"Some barrier appears to have collapsed," I record the next morning in my journal. The dream leaves me ripe with memory and feeling, the necessity of my path obsesses me and, for more than a decade, I investigate this relationship through the writing here, seeking to determine what, in the end, it has meant in my life.

Perhaps it is important to explain that I was not, in fact, B's "last protégé". She moved to Denver in 1945 after her expectations to be hired as the conductor with the Denver Symphony were disappointed. She had to live and if she could not earn a living as a conductor, she would have to teach. Her first and most treasured protégé was Carlos Moser. After him, there was Bob Nadeau and Judy Collins. There were other, lesser stars, of course. In 1949, after my audition and at the time B claimed me, Carlos had moved to New York to conduct, Bob was engaged to Lea and they were performing the Poulenc two-piano concerto around town, and Judy was slipping into disinterest and rebellion, following a different star. Some others had moved on or faded away. What more perfect timing for the introduction of a new protégé, a fresh possibility, a bright new possibility, new potential to feed the master's desire.

Still, whether fact or fiction, "The Last Protégée" blazons itself across the dream like a banner. The imperative nature of the dream voice issuing from the mouth of the scar-faced man cannot be questioned. That I am left with a somewhat daunting responsibility for completing what I have so long ago begun, is manifestly, indubitably clear.

I pick up pen and pad and prepare to re-enter that world hoping, once more, to discover through form, its purpose and therefore its meaning in my life.

Through a Prism

Foster Mother: "She was illegitimate, you know. Her father was some kind of fly-by-night musician. A pianist, I think. Probably Italian. We took her out of the orphanage, rescued her from the nuns. Then two years later, the family came, wanted to take her away. Petitioned the Church! We escaped, set sail a week before the court date. Brought her to this country and made a fresh start. We changed her birthday and renamed her Wilhemina, after our Queen."

Many were the times I regretted keeping her. She was an extremely difficult and willful child."

Theosophist: "Yes, Mrs. Wolthius came to our meetings. She was a stern woman, that one. She brought that child with her, poor little thing. She was always looking for someone to love her, fainting into our arms just to be held."

Surrogate Mother: "Yes, I helped her trace her parentage, encouraged her to find her relatives in Rotterdam. That was when she was a teenager. She made a trip there after she graduated, I think. Found her birth certificate, real name. It was enormously important for her to do so."

Disciple of Parmahansa Yogananda: "Antonia met Master in New York. He was giving a series of lectures.

She saw an ad in the newspaper and came. She was seeking guidance for her unhappy life. Many problems. Master helped her. She was deeply affected by his teachings and herself became a dedicated disciple, I believe."

Dean, Music Department, University of California, Berkeley: "Of course I discouraged her! What possibility of success had she? A woman conductor!"

Conductor, Berlin Symphony: "A most gifted musician, a most industrious student. Determined. The only woman ever allowed to study here."

Anaïs Nin: "It was Antonia's first concert of her New York Women's Symphony – it was one of the climaxes of my career as an analyst. She conducted marvelously – a demon, a force, a compelling magnificent performance – all Carnegie Hall was electrified."

Music critic, *Allgemeine Zeitung*: "Miss Brico conducted with temperament and energy and with great superiority in structural and melodious climaxes."

Olin Downs, music critic, *The Times*: "… her conceptions were always distinguished by musical impulses and knowledge. Every detail was carefully adjusted to the whole."

Friend: "We moved to Denver during the war – it was 1943, I think. Tonia's New York Symphony had folded. She had interviewed with the board of the Denver Symphony Orchestra and it seemed certain that she would be their new conductor. It failed to transpire, of course. She was devastated. We never learned why they suddenly lost interest, wouldn't talk to her. She thought it was because she was a woman. Well, we were stuck, so Tonia began advertising for piano and voice students. She made us a living. After a few months, she formed her own orchestra: the Denver Businessmen's Symphony. After a few years, I returned to New York."

DSO Board Member: "Naturally, in the beginning we were impressed; the orchestra was impressed. We had an opening ... but then, well, there were rumors ... out of New York, queer things, you know. The wives were upset. We couldn't have her, of course. Tried to put the best face on things, but she had already moved out here, you know. Very bad business all around."

Journalist, *Westword Magazine*: "At one point Brico sought out the novelist, Anaïs Nin, for some amateur psychoanalysis – which Nin provided, while privately scorning Brico as a kind of sexual predator. But in light of Nin's own neurotic eroticism and penchant for experimentation, it remains an open question as to who was preying on whom."

Mother of a protégé and friend: "Well, it was after she had bought her house – 1955, I think it was. She just up and left for Europe, leaving us to finish the move! Just like her. We all exist just to carry her train, I told Robert. I was packing up her room in the apartment when I came across the letters. They were from Anaïs Nin. I recognized the name. I shouldn't have read them, of course. I wished I hadn't the minute I saw what was in them. No, I can't say. I don't want to talk about it. I'm sorry I ever laid eyes on them."

Madame Cherry, Carmel: "Antonia? Yes, of course. She came every summer to stay, to lecture here at the Foundation. Sometimes about music, Sibelius, once or twice about Albert Schweitzer. She spent several summers with Schweitzer in Africa, you know. She idolized him, his great humanity, his knowledge and love of Bach. Once she brought a protégée who gave a recital in our hall – a sweet child, talented – her playing reminded me of Willie Kapell. Antonia had a house in Carmel that she kept rented. It was for her retirement, she said. I could never

163

imagine Antonia 'retired' somehow. An extremely talented and interesting woman; traveled, educated. She spoke nine languages, at least."

Protégé One: "She is the Immortal Beloved."

Assistant Choral Director, Denver: "Losing the Denver Opera Company was one of the great tragedies of her life. She founded the thing, gave it her time and energy! Banked on this to expand her reputation. A rotten thing for the board to do – *her* board! The second year, they just brought in a man to replace her. A man without credentials equal to hers, I might add. Certainly a man without her dedication and passion. I don't think she was ever truly appreciated in this country. Perhaps it was because she was such a domineering woman. Some people don't like that. Well, this betrayal, it was a blow to her, I can tell you. She never really got over it."

Friend: "Very sad life. She wanted so much – yearned for a fame that was large and international. Yearned to be adored. I always thought some of this stemmed from her sad childhood. In spite of her many successes, so many agonizing disappointments."

Protégé Two: "I will not speak of her. I am inflamed with hatred, swollen with pain."

Pianist: "Yes, she invited me – a special concert in Carnegie Hall. In the mid-80s, I think. Invited all the right people. Some came. I didn't go."

Bruno Walter, conductor: "I was invited, yes, I attended, out of compassion, curiosity also. Sad situation. She floundered, confused ... difficulty with her tempi, her baton. I understand she paid the musicians out of her own pocket. Extremely sad. I think she died shortly after that."

KVOD, classical station radio host: "A noble and courageous woman. What abilities she had to squeeze their best out of her musicians. Some of the most stirring concerts I ever heard. Marvelous! Yes, I did a series of interviews with her. Well, some of the information was extremely personal. I typed all of the interviews up myself and gave her to go over. She told me her housekeeper (!) scolded her for telling me about her personal traumas."

Housekeeper: "Certainly she made me her Executor. I sold things, spent money on her statue. She would have wanted it. I wanted it. Certainly I destroyed some of her papers. Nobody's business, those things!"

Concertmaster, Denver Businessmen's Orchestra: "Elegies by people she hardly knew, piped vibrato organ – it all just seemed so inappropriate for her – a passionate lover of fine music all her life. I couldn't get over it. She would have hated her funeral."

Biographer: "Her memory still survives in the minds of her many compatriots and fellow musicians … along with her many students and faithful followers worldwide. It is unfortunate that such a pivotal figure in the world of women's history should be allowed to fade away so quickly."

Protégé Three: "She is my obsession."

Bliss Among The Rodins

I continue to seek a purpose beyond what meaning I sometimes think I have found in my investigations of my life with B. This seeking leads me to track down a forgotten artist, a sculptor, now aged and infirm. I find her in San Francisco General. The interview does not go well.

I feel like a grape, bruised and dry from the summer's crush - an old depression, less purple than gray, or black, or blue. The result of burying the soul under an overload of ambition? Something else?

I should, I think, have stopped last weekend with the first interview, but in eagerness (and delusion, too), so determined to meet the crone sculptor in San Francisco. A glorious beginning. First, touring museums, happening on Fenstermacher in recital on the 4500-pipe organ at the Palace (Bach, bliss and tears among the Rodins). Unspeakable.

I should, I think, have ended the day there, but so single-minded is my desire to come home with another file for the archives, I stop by San Francisco General where I find her. Two hours writing out questions, trying to be heard, to be seen, to communicate. Such arrogance in her and such demands to hold onto all knowledge. I leave dispirited and defeated.

The weekend empties me. Dreams last night of B, her imperialistic attitudes, control, manipulations, all returning, just like the old sculptor. All making me feel small, ignorant, humiliated, like a child of ten again, and all so long past and B dead so many years. Still with such power over my emotions.

Always I think of King Lear to Cordelia, "*Better never to have been born than not to have pleased me.*" The pain stops here.

Gifts and Forgiveness

*Why do you raise your arms
instead of clasping us in them?*
~ Kafka

After the oracle, thinking long on the ineluctable ambiguity of my past and on my relationship and true feelings for B. On the mysteries of obsession and love. How, in the end, do I remember her: Tante Antonia, Dr. Brico, B, "she"? Friend or foe? An abyss of great absence?

This all draws me to thoughts of you, my dearest, but lost friend – to memories beyond forgetting. Do you remember how, at State, we pretended to be men? Poets? Wordsworth and Coleridge? How we *were* poets together for a time. And how we marveled reading Redgrave's *The Unseen Real,* and his report of Coleridge, his weather-sensitivity, his demographic, and then laughed immoderately at the idea of how *my* thighs might turn argent in bad weather?

I remember you standing in the humanities hall, you in your old suede Birkenstocks, flicking cigarette ash onto the cold concrete floor. Or, after class, sitting over our food in the Union, mopping up grease with thin napkins. The aspirin and double diet Cokes you swilled, claiming they made you high. Always searching for answers for better living through orthomolecular chemistry.

What visionaries we were then. Lapping up the romantic poets, changing our identities on a daily basis. Today Wooly and Sam, tomorrow Remedies Varo and Dora Carrington. How once, in despair, you wrote: "O my dear, where are we going in our pathetic women's lives?" Our struggles for identity, for a path.

And that December 13th, the memory of our St. Lucy's Day

Celebration: our laurel crowns, the candles and smudge sticks, the blessing wands and Santa Lucia buns. The champagne. Above all, your hennaed hair – wild, Don DeLillo *important*. Afterwards I jot down fragments for a story about you; about how your "outlaw imaginings" ignite, and you, your head aflame, run heralding creativity in the streets. You with your poet's soul and generous heart. You with your crazy dips and delusions. You with your rare and great beauty.

And then, December 14th, a different celebration, your birthday, but also the day, four years later, the Mayor of Denver proclaims "Antonia Brico Day." A constellation of feelings. The two of you, some similarities I see now, but mostly the antipodal shores of my existence where I live and relive the past, the present, and dream the future.

Here, now, exploring my feelings for you and for

her (how I seek to bind you to me!), I understand how differently (and how less) I care for her, B, Dr. Brico, my Tante Antonia. She, who desired and demanded so much.

Coda

B on a Mount of Gems

*In a dream you saw a way to
survive and you were full of joy.*
~Jenny Holzer

The ground strewn with gems, emeralds, rubies,
amber and sapphire. Sparkling with a wisdom
that has eluded me through all those decades
of mulling and sifting through memories. The dry
years of resentment, self-victimization, revolution,
involution. A revelation!

B, atop the mount, like a prophet, or conqueror,
an untouchable, and at her feet, sparkling in the sun,
a certain splendor, her gifts – gifts to which I have
refused for so long to lay claim. The dream leads to
a final sense of, if not devotion, a quick and lasting
gratitude and I remember the ripeness of those years
and cannot not, any longer, accept the decay.

For over forty decades, immured in layers of
distortion, newscasting the sad story of *her betrayal.*
But in spite of seeking, through every means, to define
the parameters of this betrayal, no image of certainty
emerges. Like a child, fearful of a superior
punishment, my finger pointed resolutely at B, at her

unreasonable demands, her "abuse," her betrayal. A text distorted, printed in reverse, seen in a funhouse mirror.

All of those initial dreams of "retailing," of B's imperatives to write the story, has, in the end, become clear. And how she urged me on, taunting me through dream after dream, unwilling to allow me the small dark luxuries of my fury and well of woundings. As though her nature endures beyond this plane, beyond life here. As though, by dying, she has taken up residence in me.

If I am honest, I will say that I did not, could not, *love* her. The differences were too great. What I can feel now, and feel deeply, is an immense gratitude for the difference her example and teachings have made in my life: the broadening cultural spectrum of lessons, exposure to the arts, the trips; the lessons of discipline to one's passion; the importance of setting goals and of holding to them, never being deflected from the course. But, most of all, the gift of music, the heart's ecstasy when the fingers sing in practice and music of The Immortals infuses the body with epiphinda glows.

So now I am finally able to lay it all to rest, although coming to this "truth" does not, in any way, diminish the emotional validity in the pages that have gone before. Everything is "true" in that sense, although who can say what part of the whole has very much to do with the facts of that time – the events, the people as they really were. Filtered through the alembic of emotion, the distillation is necessarily subjectively mine and is surely only one of a hundred different ones, were the others to write their stories. *The Last Protégée*, however, is my story and it must stand as the story of my personal and emotional truth.

But, has the telling released the teller, after all?

We hope you enjoyed *The Last Protégé* by Nancy Deeds Resler.

About the Author

Nancy Deeds Resler, was an initiator and instructor of online Humanities and creative writing classes for ten years at the University of California, Davis Extension. Before moving to the Central Valley, she co-edited and wrote restaurant reviews for Bay Food and Wine magazine. Currently she coaches creative writers and artists, edits exhibition catalogs and books on artists. She has published essays on a variety of subjects and is currently at work on a novel about the life of a talented and eccentric contemporary composer.

Ms Resler lives in California with her husband and his cat, Tom Tom.

Made in the USA
Charleston, SC
17 March 2015